Check and test

Food Technology

Design and Technology

Louise T Davies

Published by BBC Active, an imprint of Educational Publishers LLP, part of the Pearson Education Group. Edinburgh Gate, Harlow, Essex CM20 2JE

First published 2003
Reprinted 2007

Printed and bound by Ashford Colour Press,

BBC ACTI

Contents

Introduction page 4

Product development

01 Writing a design brief 6
02 Writing an outline specification 7
03 Where do new design ideas come from? 8
04 Concept development 9
05 Concept screening 10
06 Consumer preference 11
07 Analysing existing food products 12
08 Testing and evaluating products 13
09 What is sensory evaluation? 14
10 How is sensory evaluation used? 15
11 Preference tests 16
12 Discrimination tests 17
13 Star diagrams and profiling 18
14 Designing with ICT 1 19
15 Designing with ICT 2 20
16 Recipe engineering 21
17 From outline specification to final product specification 22

Food materials and components

18 Choosing the right materials 23
19 Protein 24
20 Functional properties of protein 25
21 Gluten formation 26
22 Carbohydrates 27
23 Functional properties of carbohydrates 28
24 Fats 29
25 Functional properties of fat 30
26 Colloidal systems 31
27 Sols and gels 32
28 Emulsions 33
29 Foams 34
30 Materials revision chart 35

Understanding raising agents

31 The basics of raising agents 36
32 Air as a raising agent 37
33 Steam as a raising agent 38
34 Carbon dioxide as a raising agent 39

Understanding cake making

35 The basics of cake making 40
36 Rubbing-in method 41
37 Creaming method 42
38 Melting method 43
39 Whisked method 44

Understanding pastry making

40 The basics of pastry making: shortcrust pastry 45
41 Flaky pastry 46
42 Choux pastry 47

Understanding bread making

43 The basics of bread making 48
44 Traditional bread making 49
45 Commercial bread making 50

Understanding sauce making

46 Traditional and blended sauces 51
47 Roux and all-in-one sauces 52

Nutrition

48 Nutrition 53
49 Nutrients, sources and functions 54
50 Healthy eating 55
51 Food groups and choices 56
52 Healthy eating guidelines 57

53 *Saving Lives: Our Healthier Nation* 58
54 Nutrient intakes 59
55 Nutrition throughout life 60
56 Nutritional analysis with ICT 61

Commodities

57 Meat 62
58 Meat analogues 63
59 Fish 64
60 Eggs 65
61 Milk and milk products 66
62 Cereals 67
63 Flour 68
64 Fats and oils 69
65 Sugar 70
66 Fruit and vegetables 71

Methods of cooking

67 Heat exchange 72
68 Conduction, convection and radiation 73

Health and hygiene

69 Food hygiene 74
70 Food poisoning 75
71 Food poisoning bacteria 76
72 How can you prevent food poisoning? 77
73 Food spoilage and safe storage 78
74 Safe food handling 79

Food preservation

75 Principles of food preservation 80
76 Methods of food preservation 81
77 Pasteurisation 82
78 Sterilisation 83
79 UHT 84
80 Canning 85
81 Dehydration 86
82 Freezing 87
83 Chilling 88
84 Additives 89
85 Types of additives 90

Manufacture and production

86 Planning large-scale manufacturing 1 91
87 Planning large-scale manufacturing 2 92
88 Planning and sequencing production 93
89 Critical path analysis 94
90 Scales of production 95
91 Quality assurance and quality control 96
92 What is HACCP? 97
93 How is HACCP set up? 98
94 Manufacturing using ICT 99
95 Process control 100
96 Continuous monitoring 1 101
97 Continuous monitoring 2 102
98 Packaging 103
99 Labelling 104
100 Packaging technology 105

Answers 106

About GCSE Bitesize

GCSE Bitesize is a revision service designed to help you achieve success in the GCSE exams. There are books, television programmes and a website, which can be found at **www.bbc.co.uk/schools/gcsebitesize**. It's called *Bitesize* because the revision is broken down into bite-sized chunks, making it easier to learn.

How to use this book

This book is divided into the 100 essential topics you need to know, so your revision is quick and simple. It provides a quick test for each bite-sized chunk so you can check that you know it!

Use this book to check your understanding of GCSE Food Technology.
If you can prove to yourself that you're confident with these key ideas, you'll know that you're on track with your learning.

You can use this book to test yourself:

- during your GCSE course
- at the end of the course during revision.

As you revise, you can use *Check and Test* in several ways:

- as a summary of the essential information on each of the 100 topics to help you revise those areas
- to check your revision progress: test yourself to see how confident you are with each topic
- to keep track and plan your time: you can aim to check and test a set number of topics each time you revise, knowing how many you need to cover in total and how much time you've got.

GCSE Bitesize revision materials

The GCSE Bitesize Revision: Technology website provides even more explanation and practice to help you revise. It can be found at:
www.bbc.co.uk/schools/gcsebitesize

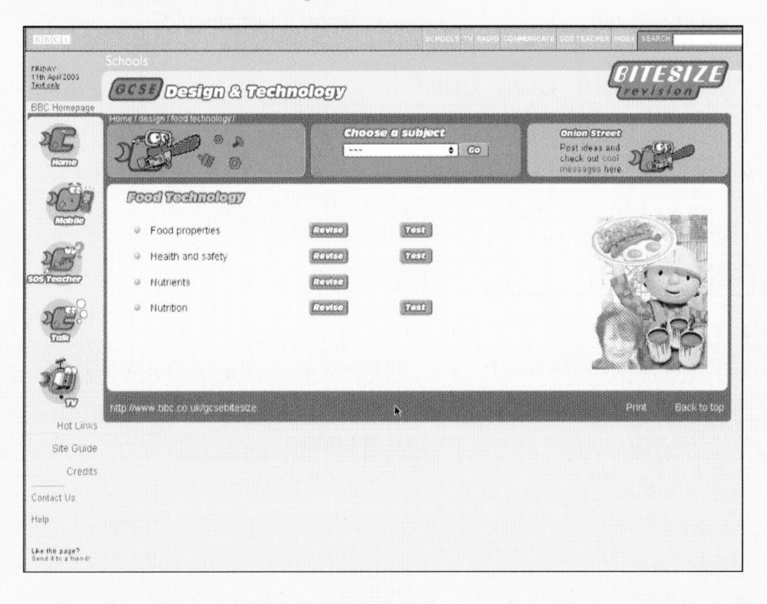

Writing a design brief

Check the facts

A design brief is a set of instructions from one person (usually the client) to a designer about what to design and make.

It should include the following **four** things about the food product:

- the nature of the food product
- where/when it will be eaten
- who will consume the product
- where it will be sold.

Writing your own brief

Sometimes you are given a brief, but writing your own design brief helps you to focus on what you are **trying to achieve** and your **priorities**.

Questioning a brief

Brief: design and make shaped chocolate novelties to sell in a zoo and theme park gift shop. It must be cheap to make large quantities of the same product.

Does the brief make sense?	What is a shaped chocolate novelty?
What am I expected to do?	Design a chocolate novelty; make it in large quantities.
What must I not do?	Design something expensive.
What will it look like when I have done it?	A chocolate novelty in a shape for a zoo/theme park – i.e. an animal shape.
What would it look like if I did it really well?	Attractive, people would want to buy/eat it.
In what other ways might I approach it?	There could be a zoo theme on the outside of the packaging, or a set of animals to collect.
Can I respond to brief in a way to surprise people?	Use different chocolate for different shapes – polar bear in white chocolate, etc.
How would I change this brief?	Not everyone likes chocolate, these could be gum or sugar or biscuit shapes.

Test yourself

1 Underline the key words in this brief:
Design and make a new salad, which looks good and appeals to customers in supermarkets. Use fruit and vegetables from different parts of plants. It should have a low-fat salad dressing to accompany it.

2 Find alternative words to the ones you have highlighted to make sure you know what they mean.

Check the facts

A food product specification is a detailed description of a product.

What is an outline specification?

Food companies develop new products from an initial brief and then, in the same way as you do at school, use market research and concept modelling to put together an **outline specification**.

It is a series of statements which describe the **possibilities** and **restrictions** of the product. Some statements are specific and some are open:

- the snack bar must have a fibre content of at least 5 g
- it can be any flavour
- the bar should be chocolate coated.

When you have completed your initial research, you should be in a position to write an outline specification.

Writing an outline specification

1 Describe the product – stating its function or purpose.

2 Use the following headings to help you with broad criteria that you will use to develop the product ideas:

- aesthetics
- costs
- ingredients
- health and safety
- environmental issues
- shelf-life.

Developing the specification

As the product is developed, modified and refined, the specification becomes more precise, until the **final product specification** is reached. This contains the finished product standards for the materials, processes, shelf-life and packaging that will be agreed by the manufacturer and the retailer.

A final product specification may include:

- the type/name of product
- the ingredients used
- details about cost
- its size or weight
- how it is made
- shelf-life (minimum and maximum).

Test yourself

1 What does the word 'specification' mean?

2 What is the difference between an outline specification and a final product specification?

3 What is meant by 'developing a specification'?

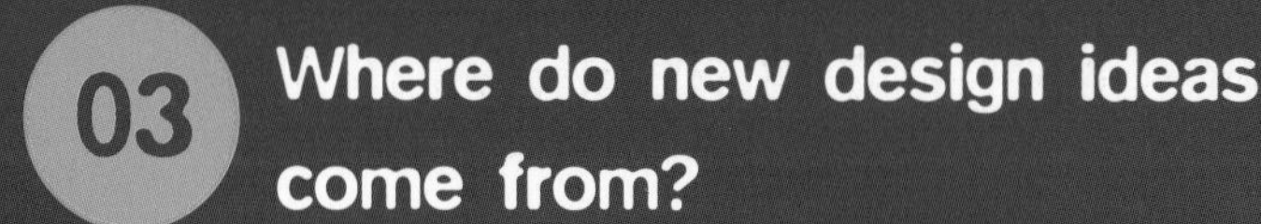

03 Where do new design ideas come from?

Check the facts

A new product is one that has never been designed and made before.

Product development is all about **ideas**. Not one big idea, but lots of different, wacky, sensible, imaginative, creative ideas; putting ingredients together that weren't associated before. From 100 ideas you might have 10 that are worth making samples of and even these might fail at the first stage.

In 1999, Campden and Chorleywood Food Research Association calculated that 7318 new food and drink products were launched in the UK. The failure rate for new food products is high – around 90% don't continue to be sold.

Why are new food products developed?

	New products are developed to:
✔	respond to people's changing tastes
✔	compete against other companies
✔	increase profits
✔	replace some products which no longer sell well.

Where do new ideas come from?

- Brainstorming
- Looking at competitors' products globally
- Analysing trends in consumers' eating habits
- Modifying existing products for specific target groups, e.g. wheat/nut-free
- Health trends, e.g. low-fat meals
- Government guidelines, e.g. *Targets for Health*
- Ethnic foods from the growth in travel overseas
- A new ingredient or process is developed
- Competitions in magazines
- Inventors (who sell ideas)
- Customer complaints
- Recipes from famous restaurants and their chefs
- Fashion trends (food can follow trends, like clothes and shoes)

Test yourself

1 Why are new foods developed?

2 What is a 'new food product'?

3 How many new food products are developed each year?

Check the facts

A concept is a general notion about a food product, around which ideas can be developed.

What is concept development?

A concept is a **starting point**, from which vague, early ideas can be made clearer, so that a product can be developed further.

A concept may be in relation to a:

- particular need
- new area of the market
- particular price band
- particular food commodity/ingredient
- new way of eating or combining foods
- rethink, improvement or update of a product.

The aim is to develop and model the idea as a **real product** – to put the ideas into practice and to think it through with real materials. This helps you to **visualise**, or **conceptualise**, the product you are aiming to develop. It gives you something objective to evaluate against during the developing and prototyping stages.

Use some of the following techniques to help you develop concepts:

- ask questions about **what the product will be like** and **who will eat it**
- evaluate a range of **existing** and **similar products**
- **get inspiration** from tried and tested ideas in recipe books from other times and cultures
- create a mood board or image board to communicate the concept, using a **visual image**
- **brainstorming**
- **attribute analysis** – look at the attributes or characteristics, e.g. texture, key flavours, appearance – use a star diagram.

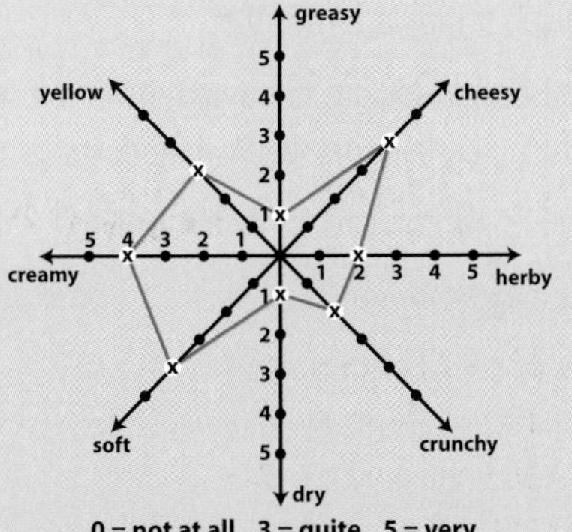

Test yourself

1 What is a 'concept'?

2 What is 'concept development'?

3 What techniques can you use to develop concepts?

Check the facts

Concept screening is the process of filtering ideas and testing the feasibility of a product so that the best ones are left for development and production.

Food companies use processes to **test** and **evaluate** a number of ideas. There are stages or decision points at which point those ideas that are not good enough are eliminated.

One example is the **innovation funnel model** used by Birds Eye Walls. This is a way of concept screening or testing the feasibility of the concept:

1 Marketing and product development people brainstorm ideas.

2 The ideas are filtered, or screened, through a number of stages, becoming fewer and more focused. They are tested to see if they are realistic.

3 The best ideas are narrowed down to one which seems most worthwhile developing.

4 This is put forward for development.

Ideas
Initial marketing and technical concepts are brainstormed

Feasibility
Finding out if the product is realistic. Concept is fine-tuned and a prototype is developed.

Capability
Work is done on the prototype to give the best product possible.

Launch
Commercial production and distribution of the product.

The development team have to think about a number of questions:

- how will it be produced?
- can it be produced using existing technology or will a new production line be needed?
- what will it cost?
- how will it be advertised?
- does it meet consumer needs?
- is it likely to sell?

The failure rate for new products is around 90 %. Companies invest a lot of time and money in product design and carry out considerable research into what consumers want and if a product is likely to be successful.

Test yourself

1 What is 'concept screening'?

2 Describe the main stages of concept screening.

3 What is an 'innovation funnel'?

4 What is the failure rate for new products?

Check the facts

Aesthetics describes the way we respond to food with our senses – sight, hearing, taste and smell.

When designing a new food product, companies need to ask:

- Is there a need?
- Will people buy it?

Aesthetics – appealing to our senses

Aesthetics play an important role in our choice and enjoyment of food. The aesthetic characteristic of food is particularly important. We all differ in the things we like or dislike. Ask your friends to name a food product they dislike and you'll find a wide variety. Ask them why and they will probably point out reasons to do with the **texture**, **taste** and **colour** of the food.

In designing food products, thinking about aesthetics is very important. To check that the food product appeals to the senses, food designers carry out a number of different types of tests during the planning and making of products. This can be **consumer preference tests** or **sensory analysis**.

Subjective tests

Any testing which relies on people's likes and dislikes is known as **subjective testing** because it varies from person to person.

Consumer preference tests

Food and packaging can be discussed as **qualitative research** by a **consumer panel**. This involves people discussing how they feel about a product during the prototype stage. It relies on people's feelings but gives a designer a good idea of how the product will be received by the public.

Test yourself

1 What is meant by 'aesthetics'?

2 What are 'subjective tests'?

3 What is a 'consumer panel'?

Analysing existing food products

Check the facts

Finding out about existing products helps you find out how successful products have been made and may stimulate new ideas.

Market intelligence

To work successfully, you must know what is new on the supermarket shelf. The product development team will buy and taste **competitors' products**.

Disassembly or attribute analysis

Existing products are often analysed during food product development to help stimulate ideas; not just ideas for the product itself, but also looking at how it is **packaged**, **presented** and **marketed**.

The food technologist is likely to analyse the existing product by **disassembly**. This technique may also be known as **attribute analysis**.

- What ingredients and processes have been used?
- How and why have they been used?
- What makes the product successful?
- Where could it be improved?
- Are there any missed opportunities that could be developed?

Test yourself

1 What is 'market intelligence'?

2 What is 'attribute analysis'?

3 Select a food product that interests you (or that you are currently working on). It may represent a new development or a familiar favourite. How many versions of this product can you find in any one supermarket? Analyse the main features of each product in order to compare them.

Check the facts

Evaluation is part of the on-going process to refine the end product. During this development a product is modelled, tested and trialled; and constantly adapted and improved.

To find out how successful a design is, you need to test it. **Compare** it with similar products yourself. Ask others to evaluate it using **sensory analysis**.

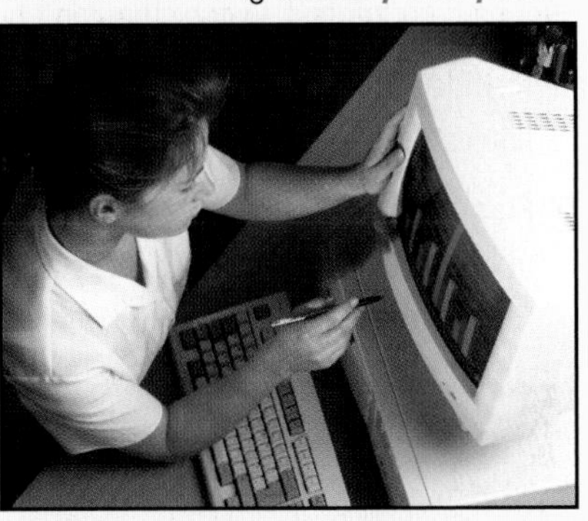

Nutritional analysis
Nutrition may be a priority consideration during product development, e.g. if the product has a particular nutritional claim, such as 'low fat'. Software is commonly used in the food industry to model and test the nutritional profile.

Sensory evaluation
Product evaluation partly relies on using human senses in scientific ways to carry out **sensory evaluation tests**. Tasting is an important evaluation tool, for example. Measurements and information from such tests will inform the designing process. There are standard tests used by the food industry (BS5929), which are performed under controlled conditions.

Preference tests are subjective tests, indicating how much a product is liked or disliked. These are useful when assessing **product acceptability** – how acceptable a product is to consumers. Manufacturers may use preference tests to evaluate their product against a competitor's.

Objective tests provide more detailed information. For instance, discrimination tests compare samples to find out whether there are any detectable differences between them, e.g. crunchiness of a product. Small amounts of slightly differing recipes can be made up as samples in order to test and compare the results for preference and against the specification.

Test yourself

1 What is 'evaluation'?

2 What is 'nutritional analysis'?

3 What are 'preference tests'?

4 What are 'objective tests'?

09 What is sensory evaluation?

Check the facts

Sensory evaluation assesses different characteristics of food, such as taste, odour and texture. 'Tasters' look at, smell and eat the food samples, recording their opinions.

How should a sensory evaluation be set up?

To ensure a fair test, tasters shouldn't be distracted or influenced in any way.

- Provide individual booths, free from cooking smells and with **controlled lighting**.
- Samples should be of the **same size**, served in identical, **plain white dishes** at the correct **temperature**; coded with **random numbers**.
- **Water** and **crackers** should be consumed between samples.

What senses are used?

The tasters focus on one attribute at a time, such as taste or appearance, and record their responses on paper or directly onto a computer.

Sight	Appearance (size, shape, colour, surface texture and presentation) is important when a consumer is deciding whether or not to purchase and eat a product.
Smell and taste	These senses work together. The tongue detects sweet, sour, salty and bitter tastes. The nose detects volatile aromas released from food.
Hearing	Sometimes a product is associated with a sound, such as the juicy crunch of an apple.
Mouthfeel or touch	When food is eaten, different sensations are felt as the food is chewed and broken up.

Test yourself

1 What is 'sensory evaluation'?

2 What senses are used?

3 How should a sensory panel be set up?

How is sensory evaluation used?

Check the facts

Companies use sensory evaluation to develop new products and check the quality of existing ones.

Sensory evaluation can be used to:

- monitor prototypes, checking that the specification or improvements are being met
- assess whether a new product is likely to be acceptable to, or popular with, consumers
- find out whether people can distinguish between different products, e.g. lower-fat products compared with traditional products
- investigate whether one product is more popular than another
- assess any improvement in consumer appeal by profiling the characteristics of a modified product against those of the original
- describe specific attributes about a product, e.g. its sweetness
- measure shelf-life by testing samples at known periods after production to see how eating quality is affected
- assess quality - maintain consistent uniform taste feature across different batches of a product, e.g. supermarket wine tasters
- carry out quality control, monitoring samples from the production line against the original specification.

Test yourself

1 Why do companies use sensory evaluation?

2 How do companies use sensory evaluation during the development of prototypes?

3 How do companies use sensory evaluation to measure shelf-life?

4 How do companies use sensory evaluation to assess quality?

11 Preference tests

Check the facts

Preference tests supply information on what people like or dislike about a product. They are subjective tests.

Paired comparison test
Tasters are asked to state which of two samples they prefer.

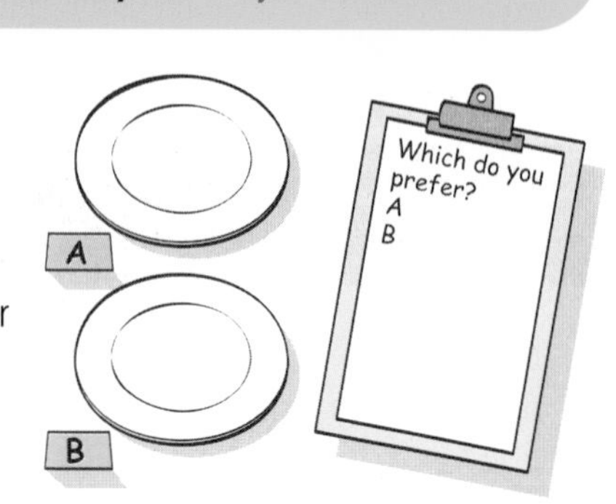

Ranking test
Tasters are asked to rank, in order of preference, a range of similar food products.

Hedonic ranking test
Products are scored on a five- or nine-point scale according to the degree of liking of a product's sensory and overall appeal. Comments are recorded, using a grid like the one below. This test should not be used to evaluate quality or specific product attributes as it is only suitable for gauging preferences.

sample	like very much	like	neither like nor dislike	dislike	dislike very much	appearance	smell	taste	texture

Test yourself

1 What is a 'paired comparison test'?

2 What is a 'ranking test'?

3 What is a 'hedonic ranking' test?

Check the facts

Discrimination tests aim to evaluate specific attributes, i.e. characteristics of products. They are objective tests.

Paired comparison

Tasters compare two samples for a specific characteristic, such as crispness.

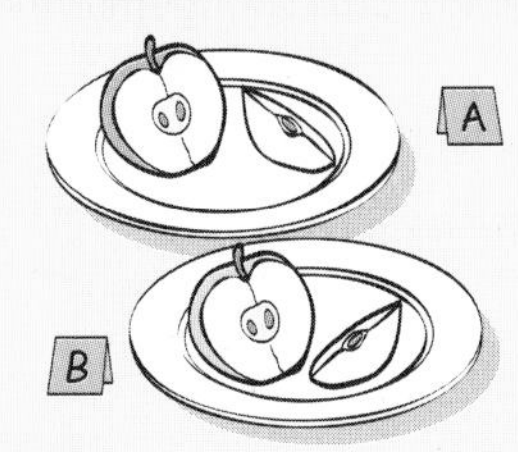

Duo trio

Given two samples, tasters are asked which one is identical to a control.

Triangle

Presented with three samples, two of which are identical, tasters are asked to identify the odd one out.

Ranking

Tasters rank samples in order for a specific characteristic, such as sweetness.

Scoring tests using scales

Samples can be scored on different scales to evaluate individual characteristics.

Test yourself

1 What are 'discrimination tests'?

2 What is a 'triangle test'?

Star diagrams and profiling

Check the facts

Profiles or star diagrams can be drawn to help describe and analyse the attributes of the product and then to test and evaluate the product against these criteria.

This method of evaluation tends to use highly-trained tasters.

You can use a different grid for each sample . . .

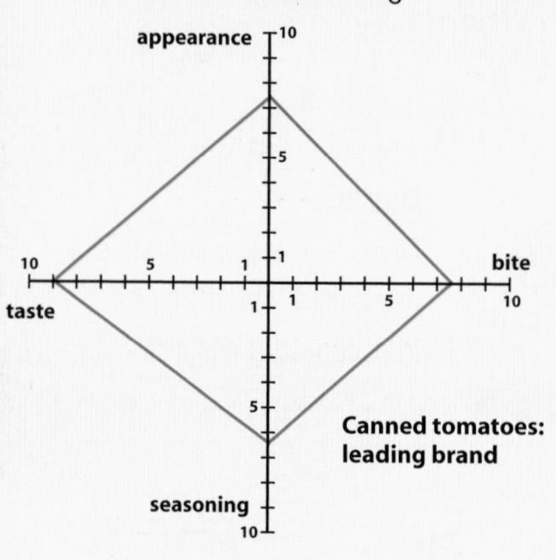

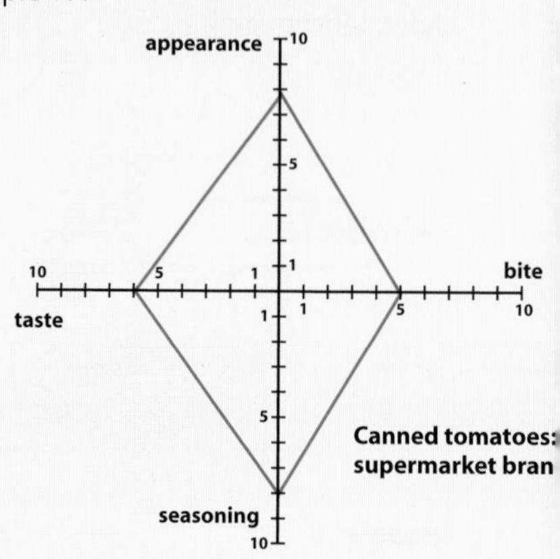

. . . or you can plot a number of results onto one grid, with a key.

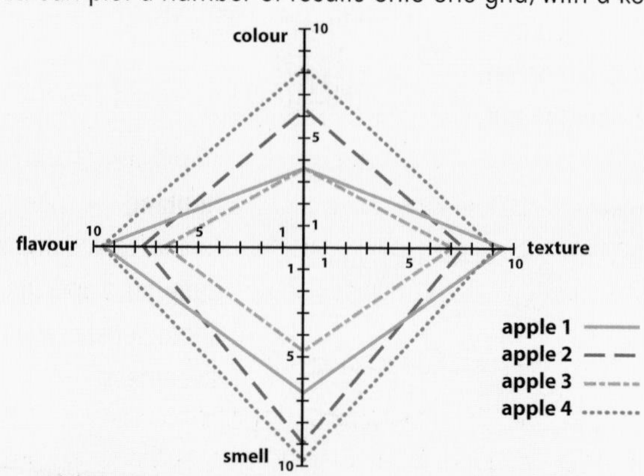

Data can be entered into a computer spreadsheet and then displayed as a star profile. You can use a six- to ten-point scale to evaluate colour, flavour, overall acceptability, volume and smell:

6 = excellent, 5 = very good, 4 = good, 3 = fair, 2 = poor, 1 = very poor.

Test yourself

1 What is another name for a star diagram?

2 What can this be used to evaluate?

Check the facts

Computers help the food industry to design and make products more efficiently. They are used throughout the food production chain, from harvesting and processing to product development and marketing.

Information and communication technology (ICT) can help food product design, development and manufacturing, in the areas of **developing**, **modelling** and **communicating ideas** to others.

Handling information

Information can be gathered, analysed and sorted or recorded and stored. This may be for research purposes, e.g. to analyse sales.

Modelling helps marketeers decide **how much to charge** for the product and helps food technologists decide on the **quantities** and **components**.

Cheese and vegetable pasty

	A	B	C	D
1	Ingredients	Quantity used	Cost/g	Total cost
2	Potatoes	200	£ 0.10	B2* C2
3	Carrots	100	£ 0.25	B3* C3
4	Cheese	125	£ 0.55	B4* C4
5	Onions	100	£ 0.30	B5* C5
6	Mixed herbs	10	£ 0.20	B6* C6
7	Leeks	125	£ 0.40	B7* C7
8				
9	Totals			sum (D2:D8)

Reducing the cost of a recipe

Computers can predict the effect of combining ingredients in **differing ratios and proportions**, e.g. the amount or type of fat. Food product developers assess the eating qualities of a particular food and use this as a **baseline**. They then use a computer to calculate how far they can reduce the cost (by adjusting the recipe) without compromising the eating quality.

Changing the nutritional content of a recipe

The ingredients and nutritional content are displayed in a **spreadsheet**. You can change the amount or type of ingredients for the recipe and the spreadsheet will recalculate and show the new nutritional content. For a cake recipe, it is possible to reduce the fat content to see how this changes the overall nutritional profile, such as calories and vitamin content.

Test yourself

1 How are computers used to help food product design?

2 How are computers used to model nutritional content?

Check the facts

ICT can be used to increase accuracy or precision, to speed up processes and to simulate a variety of functions which might otherwise require considerable time and expertise.

Making predictions

Computer software programmes can be used to model bacterial growth in food products. Tests are carried out to predict what level and type of microbacterial growth could take place. This can help the manufacturer work out **safe production**, **safe shelf-life**, and **instructions** for re-heating the product. Recipes and formulations can be analysed **microbiologically** to reduce development time and overall costs, typically by up to 70%.

Packaging design

Packaging graphics should clearly communicate **what the product is**, its **name**, company **logo**, **ingredients**, **weight** and **nutritional information**. Instructions on use and storage may also be included, along with photographs or illustrations that visually communicate something about the product. Using computers allows different colours and graphic effects to be modelled and tried out. This is less time-consuming than a graphic artist hand drawing several versions. The design can easily be altered if any details change or additional information is added.

Software packages can also be used to **design nets**. The image can then be transferred immediately onto the packaging for printing.

Virtual reality

Some companies use **virtual reality (VR)** to create supermarket shelves to see how their products might look on display. Other applications involve displaying designs for new products, such as a novelty cake.

Test yourself

1 How are computers used to predict bacterial growth?

2 How are computers used for packaging?

3 How is virtual reality used by food companies?

Check the facts

Recipe engineering adapts ideas or recipes for a commercial product that can be manufactured in large quantities.

Manufacturers use **standard recipes** for many food products. These are altered or adapted, taking care that the consumer still likes the finished product. For example, a manufacturer might try to make a jam with less sugar and replace it with another sweetner and gelling agent, without it affecting the overall quality of the final jam.

Sometimes the **ingredients**, **processes** and **handling of the food** or the **finish** of the product need to be altered. It would be very time-consuming to ice a high volume of biscuits with complex decorations by hand so a simpler decoration that can be piped quickly by machine is chosen instead.

In a recipe there may be:

- too many different stages
- too many ingredients or too many that require time-consuming preparation, e.g. fresh mushrooms
- ingredients that vary in flavour according to the time of year or are hard to find all year round, e.g. potatoes
- ingredients that are too expensive
- ingredients that need to be handled gently, e.g. fresh strawberries.

When you are adapting recipes you need to think about:

- what are the key characteristics of the product you wish to retain?
- what ingredients can be left out without losing the key characteristics?
- how can the recipe be simplified to reflect manufacturing constraints?
- any additional commercial ingredients that could be beneficial.

Test yourself

The development team have come up with an idea for a hot, potato-topped meat pie for the chilled, ready-meal market – a Christmas roast dinner pie, with all the delicious ingredients of the traditional meal. The recipe has layers of roast turkey, boiled ham, chipolatas, carrots, sprouts, stuffing, and is covered with gravy and topped with roast potatoes. Delicious but far too complicated!

1a How would you alter the recipe to simplify the ingredients and processes without losing the characteristics of the meal?

b Why would you alter it in this way?

From outline specification to final product specification

Check the facts

The exact ingredients, recipe, processes, size and HACCP procedures are defined in a written specification.

Developing a specification

While developing and modifying a food product, the **outline specification** will be continually refined until the **finished product standards** can be agreed.

Final product specifications ensure that products are made **consistently** and sets the standard of ingredients, processes and finished products. It is a checklist for **quality assurance** and **quality control** procedures.

See topic 89 on page 94 for more on HACCP.

Tolerance levels

A product specification lists **percentages** of ingredients. It includes **ingredient tolerance levels** for colour, flavour, ingredient quality, quantity and microbiological (bacteria) counts. The following recipe uses 60 % chicken flesh, but 55 –65 % is acceptable.

Ingredients for chicken nuggets (%):

60 (±5 %) chicken flesh 20 (±2 %) rusk 10 (±1 %) water 10 (±1 %) onion.

Writing a final product specification

Name of product: ______	
Finished product standards:	description of product detailed ingredients weight/size product life
Quality standards:	visual appearance taste panel results nutritional information
Processing standards:	recipe how it will be made – HACCP flow chart

Test yourself

1 What are the main steps from initial brief to final product specification?

2 What are the main headings in a final product specification?

3 What is meant by 'tolerance levels'?

Check the facts

Food materials are complex substances that behave in different ways. Food manufacturers select food ingredients with particular physical functions and working characteristics to create products.

Choosing the right materials to use for a food product will be influenced by:

- the type of product, e.g. meat, cake, cook-chill product or meal
- the retail price for the intended product, e.g. economy or luxury ranges
- the sector of the market the product will be in, e.g. frozen or canned.

Function of materials

Each ingredient in a food product is specially selected to perform a particular function: **physical**, **sensory** or **nutritional**.

Physical function

Selected because it performs a vital physical function, e.g. butter makes the end product 'short' and crumbly.

Sensory function

Selected because it gives a product a particular colour, flavour, texture, e.g. sugar provides sweetness.

Nutritional function

Selected because it has a particular nutritional content, e.g. bran has fibre.

Test yourself

1 What influences a choice of materials?

2 Why have the following ingredients been used in this biscuit recipe: flour, eggs, butter, sugar and oats – what are their sensory, nutritional and physical functions?

Check the facts

Protein is made up of chains of small units called amino acids. Proteins perform different functions in food products, depending on their physical shape and chemical structure.

Amino acids

Amino acids are compounds that contain **carbon**, **hydrogen**, **oxygen** and **nitrogen**. A few also contain **sulphur** and **phosphorus**. There are many different proteins, each one containing different amino acids joined in a particular order.

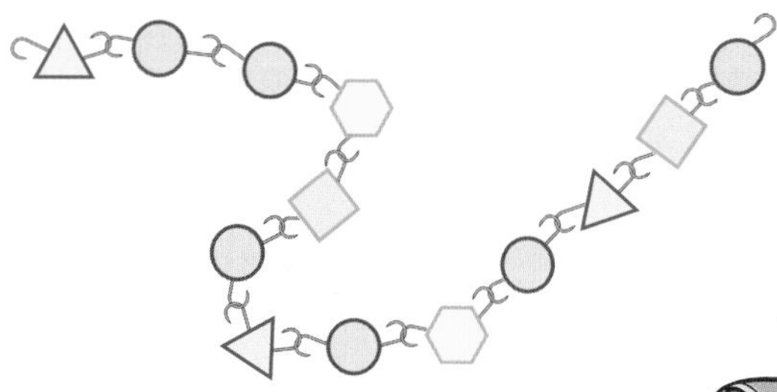

Most foods contain protein, e.g. **collagen** in meat, **gluten** in wheat flour and **albumen** in egg white.

Heating or whisking causes the protein molecules to unfold. This process is called **denaturation**. When proteins unfold from their coiled state and go on to form a solid network, they **coagulate**, or set – just like when you boil an egg.

Test yourself

1 What is protein made up of?

2 What are amino acids?

3 Why do proteins perform different functions?

4 Name **three** proteins and the foods they are from.

Check the facts

Meringue, cheese, bread and jelly are examples of food products that use the functional properties of protein.

Denaturation

Denaturation is the **change in structure** of protein molecules. The structure of protein changes due to **heat**, **salts**, **pH** or **mechanical action**, such as whisking. The process results in the **unfolding of the protein molecules**. Denaturation is a **partially-reversible change**.

For example, if a whisked egg foam is left to stand, it will collapse to form liquid egg white. The physical changes caused by whisking denature the protein, so the egg white cannot be rewhisked.

Coagulation

When egg white is cooked it changes colour and becomes firmer – it sets. This is known as **coagulation**. The heat causes the proteins to unfold from their coiled state and form a **solid, stable network**. This change is **irreversible**.

coagulation can be used for:	
thickening	Sauces or custard can be thickened by adding egg and heating.
binding	Whole raw egg adds moisture to a mixture and holds the ingredients together. As the food is heated, the egg coagulates and keeps the product whole.
coating	Egg enables coatings, such as breadcrumbs, to stick to the surface of a product and form a protective barrier during cooking.
cheese production	Rennin (enzyme from a calf's stomach) is added to milk, which causes the protein casein to clot, producing curds (solid) and whey (liquid).
yoghurt production	Milk is coagulated and soured by lactic acid produced by adding harmless bacteria

Test yourself

1 What is 'denaturation'?

2 What is 'coagulation'?

3 How is this functional property of coagulation used in food products?

Gluten formation

Check the facts

Two proteins, gliadin and glutenin, are found in wheat flour. They form gluten when mixed with water.

Gluten is strong, elastic and forms a **3D network** in dough. When bread is made, kneading helps to develop the gluten, this means it **untangles the gluten strands and aligns them**. Gluten helps gives structure to the bread. When it cooks, gluten traps gases that expand as it is heated, holding the risen loaf and giving it an open texture.

The amount and type of protein present depends on the flour type and quality. Strong flour contains a maximum of 17 % protein; plain flour, 10 %; and weak or soft flour, 8 %. Products that require short or crumbly textures, such as biscuits and cakes, use flours with a lower protein content.

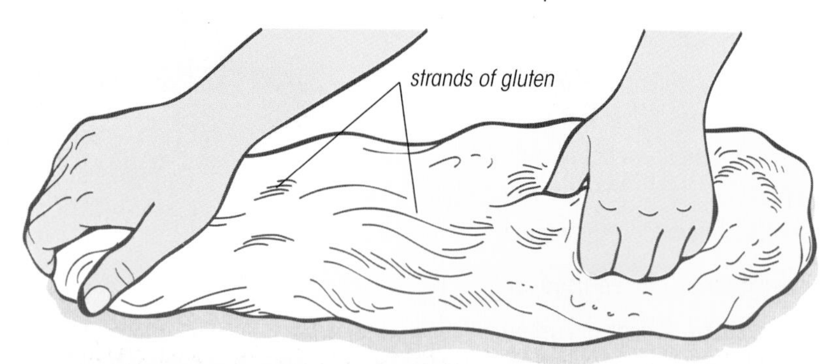

Test yourself

1 How is gluten formed?

2 What is meant by 'developing the gluten'?

3 What does gluten do?

Check the facts

Carbohydrates can be divided into three main groups: monosaccharides, disaccharides and polysaccharides, according to the size of the molecule.

Monosaccharides

These are the simplest carbohydrate molecules, e.g. glucose, fructose and galactose.

Disaccharides

These are formed when two monosaccharide molecules join together with the **elimination of one molecule of water**, e.g. sucrose (glucose and fructose), lactose (glucose and galactose), and maltose (two molecules of glucose).

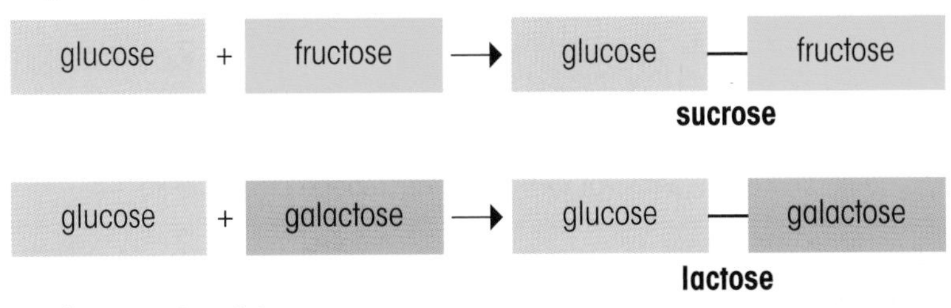

Polysaccharides

These are made up of many monosaccharide molecules, joined together, e.g. starch, glycogen, cellulose and pectin.

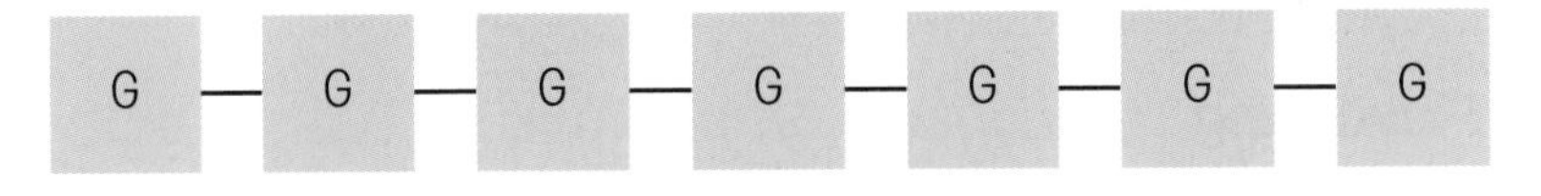

Carbohydrates perform different functions in food products. They:

- help cause the colour change of bread, toast and bakery products
- contribute to the chewiness, colour and sweet flavour
- thicken products, such as sauces and custards
- can act as a preservative, e.g. jam.

Test yourself

1 What are monosaccharides?

2 What are disaccharides?

3 What are polysaccharides?

Check the facts

Sugars and starches change when heated, giving them different properties.

Dextrinisation

Dextrin is formed when foods containing **starch** are baked or roasted (using a dry heat). When baked, grilled or roasted, the colour, flavour and smell changes, e.g. toast, bread and croissants. This is a **reaction between protein and a reducing sugar**, called the **Maillard reaction**. These **polymerise** to form complex, brown-coloured compounds, called dextrins.

Caramelisation

When sucrose is heated above its melting point it changes to **caramel**, giving confectionery a characteristic chewiness, sweetness and flavour.

Gelatinisation

When starch is mixed with water and heated, the starch granules swell, absorbing the liquid. This thickens the mixture. On cooling, **a network** holds the liquid and a gel forms, for example, blancmange and mousse.

starch molecules swelling

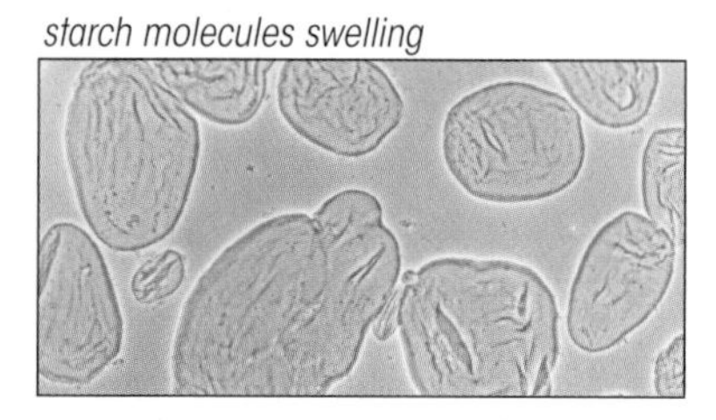

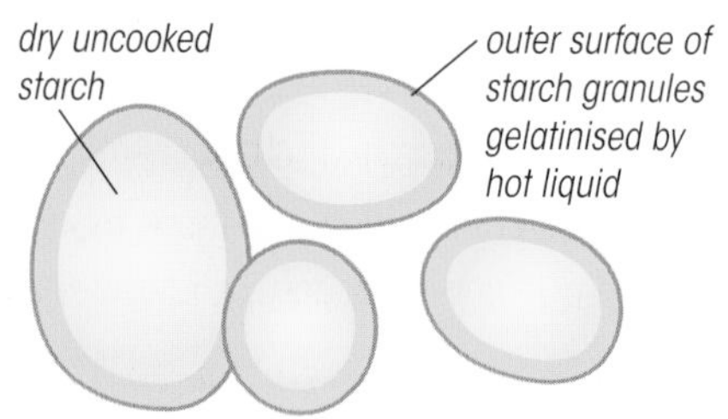

Flavouring

Sugar, e.g. sucrose, changes the sweetness and mouthfeel/touch of the product. It is used to flavour drinks, cakes and confectionery.

Preservative

In high concentrations, sugar can prevent the growth of micro-organisms. This preserving quality is used in jam, marmalade and some canned fruit.

Test yourself

1 What is 'dextrinisation'?

2 What is 'caramelisation'?

3 What is 'gelatinisation'?

Check the facts

Fats are made up of fatty acids and glycerol. They are either saturated or unsaturated, depending on the proportions of the different types of fatty acids they contain.

Fats are composed of fatty acids and glycerol:

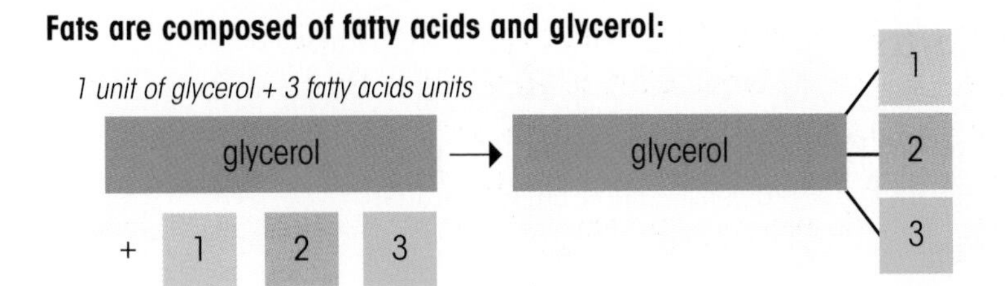

A fatty acid is made up of a **chain of carbon atoms**, with a **methyl group** at one end and an **acid group** at the other. Each carbon atom in between has either one or two hydrogen atoms attached. If the fatty acid has all the hydrogen atoms it can hold, it is said to be **saturated**.

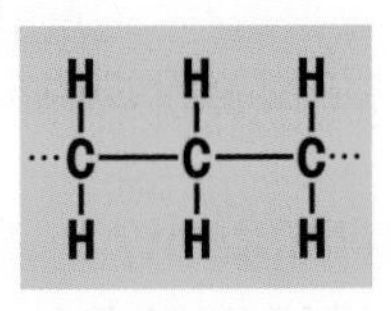

If some of the hydrogen atoms are missing and have been replaced by a **double bond** between the carbon atoms, then the fatty acid is said to be **unsaturated**. If there is one double bond, the fatty acid is known as a **monounsaturated fatty acid**. If there is more than one double bond then the fatty acid is known as a **polyunsaturated fatty acid**.

All fats contain both saturated and unsaturated fatty acids but are usually described as saturated or unsaturated according to the proportions of fatty acids present. For example, butter is often described as a saturated fat because it has more saturated fatty acids than unsaturated fatty acids.

Most unsaturated fats are **liquid at room temperature**, are usually of **vegetable** origin, and are commonly known as **oils**. They can be hardened by a process known as **hydrogenation**. Hydrogenated vegetable oils are frequently used in the manufacture of cakes, biscuits and bakery products.

Test yourself

1 What are fats composed of?

2 What is the difference between a monounsaturated fatty acid and a polyunsaturated fatty acid?

3 What is 'hydrogenation'?

Functional properties of fat

Check the facts

Fats are used for shortening, foam formation, flakiness, glazing and to increase shelf-life. Solid fats become oils at different temperatures, which is useful for different food products.

Shortening

In shortcrust pastry, biscuits and shortbread, **fat coats the flour particles**, preventing them from absorbing water. This **reduces gluten development**, giving them a characteristic, short, crumbly texture.

Different fats can be used for shortening to produce different effects. Vegetable fats are suitable because of their low water content, margarine gives a golden colour product, and butter gives a distinctive flavour.

Plasticity

All fats have unique characters, e.g. they don't melt at fixed temperatures, but **over a range**. This property is **plasticity**. Some products have lower melting points so they can pour or spread straight from the fridge, e.g. oil and margarine.

Aeration

Products, e.g. cakes, need **air incorporated** into the mixture to give a well-risen, light texture. When fat, e.g. butter, is **creamed** with sugar, small air bubbles are incorporated, forming a stable foam.

Flakiness

Flaky and puff pastry use fat to help **separate layers** of gluten and starch formed in the dough. The fat melts during cooking, leaving minute layers. The liquid present **produces steam** which evaporates and causes the layers to rise. The fat prevents the layers from sticking together.

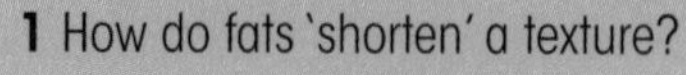

Test yourself

1 How do fats 'shorten' a texture?

2 What is meant by 'plasticity'?

3 How does fat help to aerate a food product?

Check the facts

The functions of colloidal systems can be used to give structure, texture and mouthfeel to many products.

Colloids are formed when one substance is **dispersed** through another, but does not combine to form a solution. The dispersed substance is called the **disperse phase** and is suspended in the **continuous phase**. For example, in egg white foam, air bubbles (disperse phase) are trapped in the egg white (continuous phase), resulting in a foam.

Most colloids are stable, but the two phases may separate over a period of time due to an increase in temperature or by physical force. They may also become unstable when frozen or heated, especially if they contain an emulsion of fat and water.

Main types of colloidal system

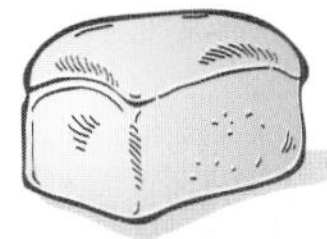

colloidal system	state of phase	examples
sol	solid disperse phase liquid continuous phase	uncooked custard unset jelly
gel	liquid disperse phase solid continuous phase	jelly, jam
emulsion	liquid disperse phase liquid continuous phase	mayonnaise, milk
solid emulsion	liquid disperse phase solid continuous phase	butter, margarine
foam	gas disperse phase liquid continuous phase	whipped cream whisked egg-white
solid foam	gas disperse phase solid continuous phase	meringue, bread, cake, ice cream

Test yourself

1 How are the functions of colloidal systems used in food products?

2 How are colloids formed?

3 Name **three** types of colloidal systems.

Sols and gels

Check the facts

Colloids are formed when one substance is dispersed through another, but doesn't dissolve to form a solution. A sol is a liquid colloid. When heated and cooled, it forms a solid gel.

A sol is a mixture in which **solid particles are dispersed in a liquid phase** (a liquid colloid). Sometimes the mixture needs to be heated and stirred. When it cools, the sol changes into a **gel**, which is solid rather than liquid.

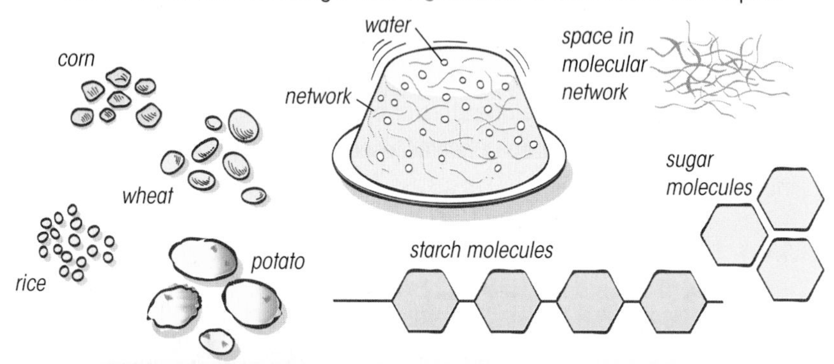

Protein and starch can be used to produce a sol or gel.

When making jelly, gelatine (protein) is dispersed into a liquid and heated to form a sol. As the sol cools, protein molecules unwind forming a network that traps water and forms a gel.

When making a sauce, cornflour (starch) is mixed with water and heated. The starch granules absorb water and the mixture becomes thick. On cooling it forms a gel.

Other types of gels are formed with **pectin** and **agar**. If a gel is allowed to stand for a time, it starts to 'weep'. This is **syneresis**.

Gelatine is a protein which is extracted from collagen, present in **connective tissue** in meat. When gelatine is mixed with warm water, the gelatine protein molecules start to **unfold**. On cooling, a stable network is formed, trapping the liquid. Gelatinisation is reversible – if you heat the gel again, it will revert back to liquid.

Test yourself

1 What is a 'sol'?

2 What is a 'gel'?

3 What is meant by 'syneresis'?

Check the facts

When water and oil are mixed together, they form an emulsion – they do not mix permanently. If it is left to stand, the oil will rise to form a separate layer on top of the water.

An example of an emulsion is French dressing. Oil and vinegar are immiscible – they will not mix together.

As emulsions separate, an emulsifying agent is used to help the oil and water phases to mix.

Emulsifying agents

A **stable emulsion** is formed when two immiscible liquids are held in a stable state by a third substance, called an **emulsifying agent**. For example, mayonnaise is a stable emulsion of oil and vinegar, when egg yolk (lecithin) is used as an emulsifying agent.

An emulsion may be:

- **oil-in-water** – small oil droplets are dispersed through water, e.g. milk or mayonnaise
- **water-in-oil** – small water droplets are dispersed through oil, e.g. butter or margarine (a solid emulsion).

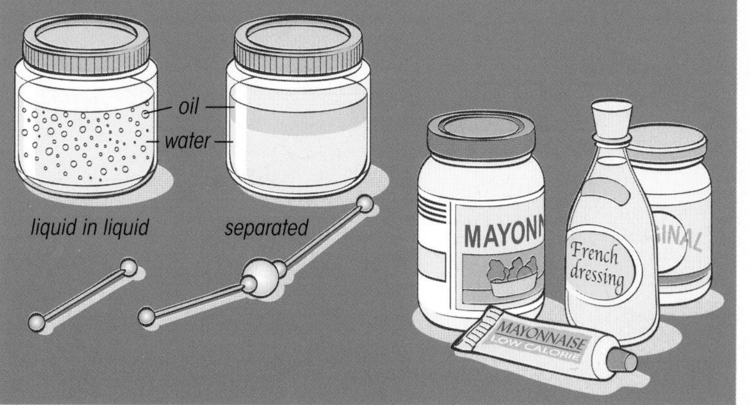

Test yourself

1 What is an 'emulsion'?

2 What is meant by 'immiscible'?

3 What are emulsifying agents and what do they do?

Check the facts

Foams are made up of small bubbles of gas (usually air) dispersed in a liquid.

Examples of a foam are whisked egg white and whipped cream.

As **liquid** egg white (or liquid cream) is whisked, **air bubbles are incorporated**. The mechanical action causes **proteins to unfold and form a network**, which traps the air bubbles and forms a foam.

If the product is **heated**, **protein coagulates** and **sets the structure** of the foam. This is a solid foam. It is possible to see air bubbles set in cooked meringue, bread and cake.

Test yourself

1 What is a 'foam'?

2 What happens when a foam is heated?

food material	physical functions	working characteristics	examples
starch			
corn flour, wheatflour, potatoes, modified starches	bulking:	starch granules swell when moisture is added	cakes, pastries, biscuits
	gelling agent:	starch granules swell when heated and gelatinise, forming a gel	gravies, sauces, custard
	thickening agent:	modified starch thickens with liquid and agitation	instant desserts, whipped cream, yoghurts, soups
sugar			
sugar, glucose syrup, honey, concentrated fruit juice	sweetens:	caramelises when heated	sweets, cold sauces
	adds colour and browning:	browns when heated – the 'Maillard reaction'	cakes, biscuits, toast, bread
	flavouring:	sweet flavour when mixed with other foods	chocolate, yoghurts, jams, desserts
	aeration:	traps air when beaten with fat when cooking delays coagulation so that the mixture rises before setting	cake mixes, gingerbread, cheesecakes
fat			
vegetable oil, animal and vegetable fat, low-fat spreads, cream	adds colour and flavour:	browning	roast and fried foods
	aeration:	traps air when beaten with sugar	cakes, mixes, ice cream
	lubricating:	moistens surfaces/mixtures, melts when heated	on bread, pate, salad dressings
	plasticity/softness:	shorten mixture/texture	biscuits, pastries
	binding:	holds ingredients together	flapjacks, biscuits
protein			
eggs, flour, milk, cream	provides structure and shape:	setting and coagulation, it hardens when heated	bread, eggs, flans, pie fillings, sauces, meatballs, coatings
	aeration:	traps air when whisked producing a foam	meringue, cakes, mousse

The basics of raising agents

Check the facts

Raising agents produce gases which expand on heating.

To make some mixtures rise and have a light texture, (such as cakes and bread) a gas must be introduced before baking. Gas expands when heated and causes the mixture to rise. As it is heated further it sets to form a firm structure, containing a network of tiny holes left by the expanded gases.

There are three gases which make food mixtures rise:

- **air** (a mixture of gases)
- **steam** (water in a gaseous state)
- CO_2.

Raising agents fall into two main categories:

- **mechanical**, such as whisking
- **chemical**, such as baking powder.

Test yourself

1 What are 'raising agents'?

2 Name **three** gases that make food mixtures rise.

Air as a raising agent

Check the facts

Air can be incorporated into a mixture by sieving, creaming, whisking and beating, folding and rolling and rubbing in.

Sieving

When flour is sieved, air becomes trapped between its fine particles. **Example:** pastry.

Creaming

When fat and sugar are creamed together, air bubbles are trapped. This changes the colour of the mixture from yellow to pale cream. **Example:** cakes.

Whisking and beating

Egg white is capable of holding up to seven times its own volume of air, due to the ability of egg protein to stretch. Whole egg traps a large volume of air when whisked.

Example: batters, meringues and cakes.

Folding and rolling

Air is trapped between layers and is sealed in. During baking, it expands and the fat melts, leaving a space that is filled with steam, which causes the layers to rise.

Example: flaky pastry.

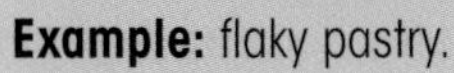

Rubbing in

Air is trapped as fat is rubbed into the flour.

Example: pastry and scones.

Test yourself

1 Name **three** ways that air can be added to a mixture.

2 How is air added to the following food products – flaky pastry, scones, meringue, cakes?

Steam as a raising agent

Check the facts

Water vapour or steam expands up to 1600 times its original volume, and is therefore an effective raising agent.

During baking, steam is produced from the liquid present in a mixture, but it is slower to react than gas expansion. Steam only works as a raising agent in mixtures:

- that contain a **lot of liquid** – e.g. batters (yorkshire pudding), choux pastry, flaky pastry
- that are **cooked at high oven temperatures** to bring the liquid rapidly to boiling point.

When the liquid in the mixture reaches boiling point, steam is given off. The steam forces its way up through the mixture, causing it to stretch and rise. The mixture cooks and sets in the risen shape, with large pockets of air left after the steam has escaped. It produces an open and often uneven texture.

Steam is often combined with other raising agents:

- air and CO_2 (cakes and bread)
- air (short-crust and flaky pastry).

Test yourself

1 Why is steam an effective raising agent?

2 What **two** things does steam need to work well as a raising agent in mixtures?

Carbon dioxide as a raising agent

Check the facts

Carbon dioxide (CO_2) is incorporated into mixtures by using chemical raising agents, such as baking powder, or biological raising agents, such as yeast. Yeast is a living organism which gives off CO_2 during fermentation.

Chemical raising agents

These are powders that require **liquid** and **heat** to produce CO_2 gas. They are used in small quantities and must be measured accurately.

Bicarbonate of soda has an unpleasant flavour and is used in recipes where it can be disguised, such as ginger cake.

Bicarbonate of soda plus acid is used when bicarbonate of soda can't be disguised as acid, e.g. cream of tartar or lemon, stops the unpleasant flavour.

Baking powder is a commercial mix of bicarbonate of soda and acid.

Biological raising agents

A yeast dough needs to **rise** or **prove**. The yeast cells multiply by **budding**, which requires energy (obtained by **fermenting** carbohydrate in the dough).

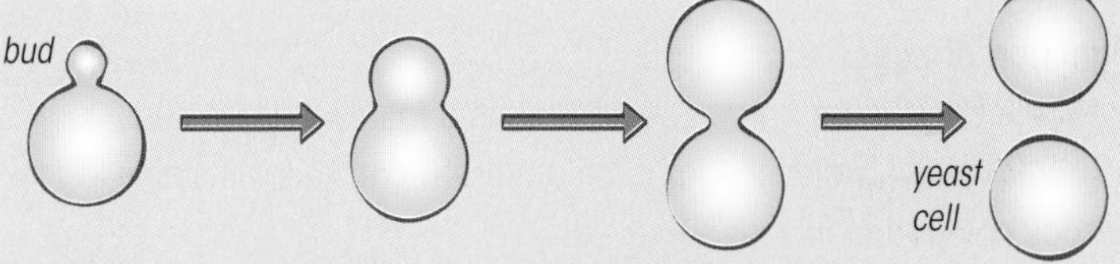

Fermentation produces CO_2 gas, which causes the dough to rise.

For successful fermentation:

Warm temperatures are needed (25–29 °C). Too much heat kills yeast, and too cold makes the fermentation slow.

Moisture, such as milk, water or egg, is needed.

Food, such as sugar and flour, provide the yeast with food to grow.

On baking, CO_2 gas expands and the dough rises. As the temperature rises, yeast activity stops and the dough sets as the **gluten coagulates**.

Test yourself

1 How is carbon dioxide incorporated into mixtures?

2 What is 'baking powder'?

3 How does yeast make a bread dough rise?

4 What happens when bread is baked?

Check the facts

Cakes are classified according to the method used for making them. The four main methods of cake making are rubbing in, creaming, melting and whisked. The ratio and type of ingredients are different for each.

Each ingredient has a specific function. The main ingredients for cake making are **fat**, **sugar** (may also be syrup or treacle), **eggs**, **flour**, **raising agent**, **liquid**, and **flavourings**.

Function of fat:

- **foam** – holds tiny air bubbles, which create texture and volume
- **shortening** – produces a short crumb or rich texture
- adds colour and flavour
- increases the shelf-life.

Function of sugar:

- **foam** – with fat, helps to hold air in the mixture
- sweetens and adds flavour.

Function of eggs:

- **foam/coagulation** – traps air and forms a foam when beaten
- **emulsifying** – holds the fat in an emulsion and keeps it stable
- adds colour and flavour.

Function of flour:

- **foam/coagulation** – as a cake is heated, protein in the flour (gluten) coagulates and sets the structure of the foam.
- **gelatinisation** and **dextrinisation** (browning)

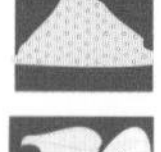

Function of a raising agent:

- makes cake light and causes mixture to rise.

Function of liquid:

- produces steam to help the mixture rise during baking
- combines with the protein in the flour to form gluten.

Test yourself

1 Name **three** different methods of cake making.

2 Why do these methods of cake making produce different cakes?

3 What are the main ingredients used in cakes?

Check the facts

The rubbing-in method produces dry, open cakes with a short shelf-life, such as fruit cake, rock cakes and scones.

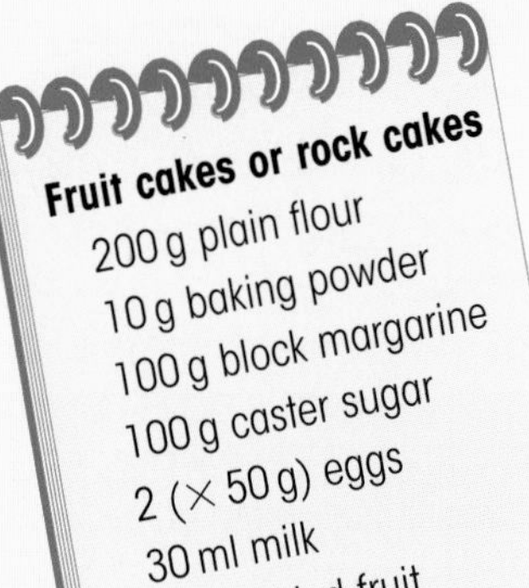

Ratio – half fat to flour or less.

Procedure

Fat is rubbed into the flour with the fingertips until it resembles breadcrumbs, before other ingredients are added to make a soft dough.

rub fat into flour

add liquid

knead gently

Test yourself

1 What is the 'rubbing-in' method?

2 What is the rubbing-in method used for?

3 What are the features of the cakes that are made by this method?

4 What is the ratio of fat to flour?

Creaming method

Check the facts

The creaming method produces fine, light cakes, such as victoria sandwich, Madeira cake, sponge buns.

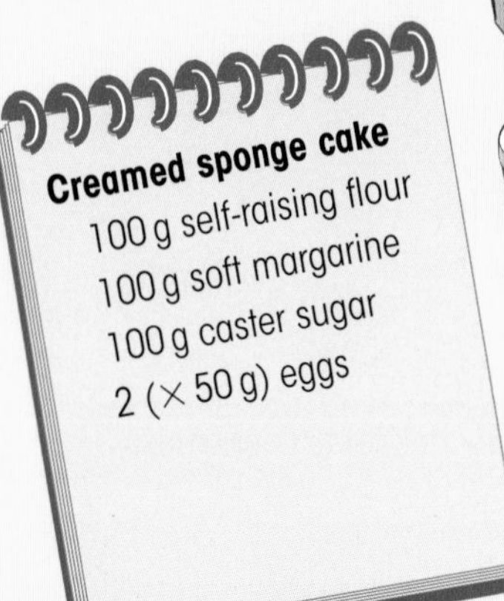

Ratio – equal ingredients according to the weight of the eggs.

Procedure

The fat and sugar are creamed together with a spoon or mixer until the mixture is white and airy. The eggs are added slowly, beating well and the flour is folded gently in, producing a mixture that falls easily from the spoon.

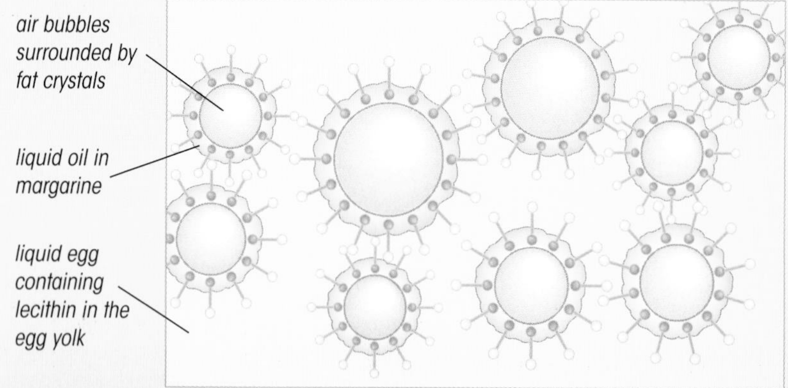

Test yourself

1 What is the 'creaming' method?

2 What is the creaming method used for?

3 What are the features of the cakes that are made by this method?

4 What is the ratio of ingredients?

Check the facts

The melting method produces soft, sticky, moist cakes that have a long shelf-life, such as gingerbread, flapjacks and brownies.

Gingerbread

- 200 g plain flour
- 5 ml bicarbonate of soda
- 10 ml ground ginger
- 5 ml mixed spice
- 100 g margarine
- 150 g black treacle
- 125 ml milk
- 2 (× 50 g) eggs
- 50 g golden syrup

Ratio – half or less fat to flour; high proportion of sugar.

Procedure

The fat is melted in a saucepan with the treacle, syrup and sugar, before the other ingredients are added, to make a thick batter.

Test yourself

1 What is the 'melting' method?

2 What is the melting method used for?

3 What are the features of the cakes made by this method?

4 What is the ratio of fat to flour?

Check the facts

The whisked method produces very light, soft cakes with a short shelf-life, such as swiss roll, sponge drops, sponge flan and sponge sandwich.

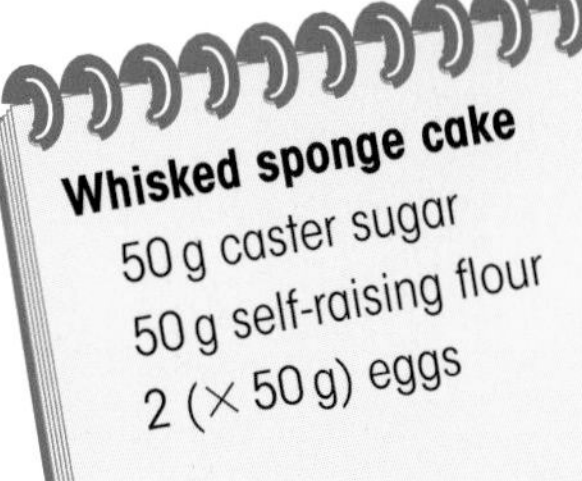

Ratio – half the amounts of sugar and flour to the weight of the eggs.

Procedure

The eggs and sugar are whisked together until the mixture has doubled in volume and the whisk leaves a trail on the top of the mixture. The flour is then gently folded into the mixture.

Test yourself

1 What is the 'whisking' method?

2 What is the whisking method used for?

3 What are the features of the cakes made by this method?

4 What is the ratio of ingredients?

40 The basics of pastry making: shortcrust pastry

Check the facts

Three common types of pastry are shortcrust, flaky and choux. They are quite different because of the way that they are made and the proportion of ingredients used.

The main ingredients used for pastry are **flour**, **fat** and **water**. Sometimes **egg** and **flavourings** are also added.

Function of flour:
- soft plain flour is used for shortcrust pastry to give it a **short crumb**
- strong flour is used in choux and flaky pastry as it contains more gluten – this is needed to make the **dough** and give the **pastry elasticity**.

Function of fat:
- **shortens** the mixture in shortcrust
- **traps air** between the layers in flaky pastry
- adds colour and flavour.

Function of water:
- the use of boiling water in choux pastry gelatinises the starch causing the **dough to thicken**
- it binds the ingredients together
- it develops the gluten in flaky and choux pastry.

Shortcrust pastry

This produces a short-crumb, light and crisp pastry used for pasties, pies and tarts.

Ratio – half fat to flour.

Procedure

The fat is rubbed into the flour with tips of fingers until it resembles fine breadcrumbs. The water is added to make a soft dough.

Test yourself

1 Name **three** types of pastry making.

2 What are the main ingredients for making pastry?

3 What is shortcrust pastry used for?

Flaky pastry

Check the facts

This recipe produces a short, crisp, layered pastry used for turnovers, cream horns, eccles cakes, and sausage rolls.

Flaky pastry
200 g strong plain flour
pinch of salt
150 g fat mixture – white fat with butter or hard margarine
2 tsp lemon juice
cold water to mix

Ratio – two-thirds to three-quarters fat to flour

Procedure

A dough is made by rubbing some of the fat into the flour and mixing it with water. The dough is then rolled out. The remaining fat is added and then folded into layers repeatedly.

Test yourself

1 What is flaky pastry used for?

2 What is the difference between flaky pastry and short crust pastry?

Check the facts

This produces a light, airy, crisp, hollow pastry case that is ideal for filling with cream or savoury fillings and is used to make eclairs, profiteroles and cheese puffs.

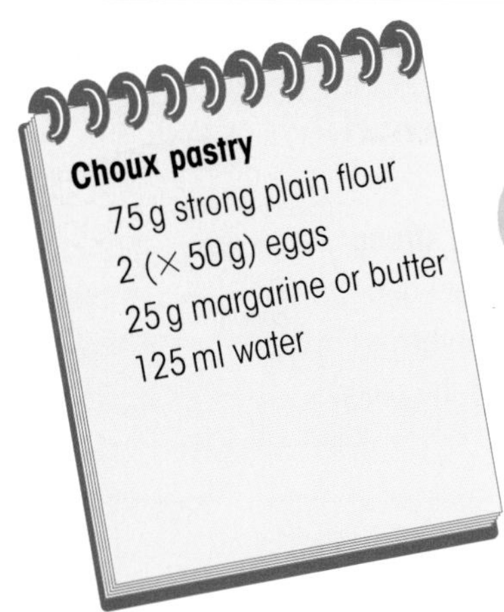
Choux pastry
75 g strong plain flour
2 (× 50 g) eggs
25 g margarine or butter
125 ml water

Ratio – third fat to flour; high proportion of water.

Procedure

The fat and water are melted and heated to a rolling boil. The flour is added and heated to form a roux (thick sauce). Once the mixture has cooled slightly, the eggs are beaten gradually into the mixture.

Test yourself

1 What is choux pastry used for?

2 How is choux pastry made?

The basics of bread making

Check the facts

Bread has been a staple food for thousands of years. Originally it was made with crushed grains of rye or barley. Today it is the main product made from wheat flour.

The four essential ingredients for bread are **flour**, **yeast**, **liquid** and **salt**.

Function of ingredients for bread

Flour
The type of flour used in bread making is **strong wheat flour**. This can be white, wholemeal or a mixture. The flour is high in **gluten**, which helps produce a very elastic dough and helps the bread to rise well, with a light, open texture.

Liquid
Water is usually used, although milk may be used for some mixtures, such as sweet dough. The liquid should be lukewarm (22–35 °C) to aid fermentation. Adding the right amount of liquid is important.

Yeast
Fresh, dried and easy-blend active yeast are different types of raising agent. **Vitamin C** is added to easy-blend active yeast to speed up fermentation.

Salt
Added at a ratio of 2 % of the flour, salt strengthens the gluten, controls the yeast and gives flavour.

Sugar
Sugar is added to sweet or rich yeast doughs.

Fat
A small amount of fat is added to enhance the colour and flavour of the dough and increase the shelf-life of the product.

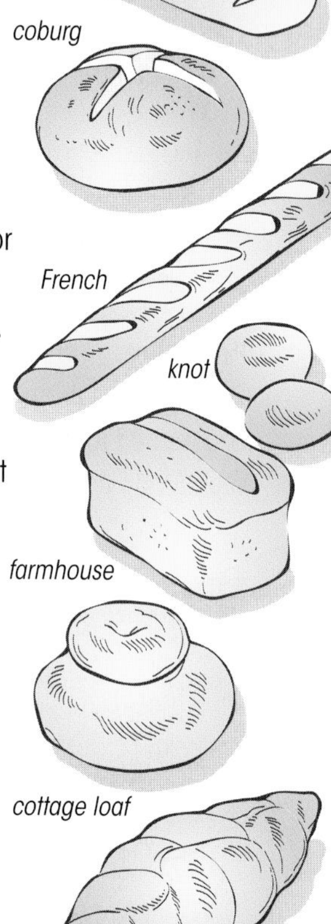

Test yourself

1 What are the main ingredients of bread?

2 What is the purpose of the yeast?

3 What is the purpose of the salt?

Check the facts

Traditional bread making involves mixing the dough, fermentation and baking. Commercial production uses bulk fermentation, activated dough development and the Chorleywood bread process.

There are five stages:

1 **Mixing**
Flour, salt and fat are mixed with yeast and the liquid to form a stiff but pliable dough. This is kneaded thoroughly for about 10 minutes to develop the gluten.

2 **Fermentation**
The dough is left to stand for 1–2 hours to rise. The yeast produces CO_2 gas, which causes the dough to rise, giving it a sponge-like, cellular structure.

3 **Knocking back**
The dough is thoroughly kneaded to release some of the gas and distribute the remaining gas bubbles, for a more evenly textured bread without large air holes

4 **Shaping and proving**
The dough is shaped into the final dough, e.g. a loaf or rolls, and left to prove or rise again before baking.

5 **Baking**
The dough is baked at a high temperature and it rises before the yeast stops working. The heat sets the structure.

Test yourself

1 What is meant by 'fermentation'?

2 What is meant by 'knocking back' the dough?

3 What is meant by 'proving'?

Commercial bread making

Check the facts

Bread factories now produce 78 % of all bread consumed. Ten million loaves are consumed every day.

Some commercial bread making is very similar to the traditional method.

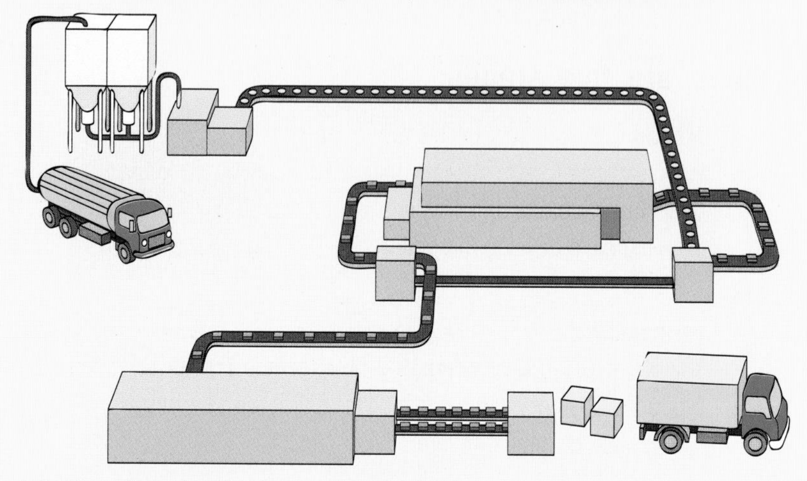

Method 1: bulk fermentation

This is the same as traditional bread making – a large quantity of dough is made and left to ferment for three hours.

Method 2: activated dough development

A **bread improver** is added to the dough. This produces bread quickly without the need to leave the dough for long periods or use heavy mixing.

Method 3: the Chorleywood process

This method was developed in 1961. The first fermentation stage is replaced with intense mixing of the dough, which rapidly stretches the gluten. The advantages of this method are that it:

- reduces factory space and time needed for bulk fermentation
- produces higher yields and reduces costs
- decreases the staling rate
- produces better quality bread.

Test yourself

1 What is meant by 'bulk fermentation'?

2 What is the 'Chorleywood process'?

3 What are the advantages of the Chorleywood process?

Check the facts

Sauces are used to add colour, flavour, moisture and nutritive value to food. There are many different types of sweet and savoury sauces. The properties and characteristics of each sauce depend on the ingredients and how it is made.

Sauces can be **thickened** in the following ways:

- by adding **starch** (white sauce or custard)
- by using a **puree of fruit** (apple sauce, raspberry sauce) or **vegetables** (tomato and onion)
- by using **eggs** (egg custard).

Many sauces are made by adding **starch**, such as wheat flour, cornflour or arrowroot to a liquid. These thicken when heated by **gelatinisation**. **Modified starch** is also sometimes used in commercial manufacture. It has been chemically changed so it may not need to be heated (e.g. instant desserts), and will not separate in frozen products.

Blended sauces

Features

A simple sauce made from cornflour or arrowroot, with milk, meat stock, fruit juice or other liquids. It has a pouring consistency and is used for custard, gravy and glazes.

How to make a blended sauce

The starch is mixed or blended with a small amount of liquid. The remaining liquid is heated, stirred into the mixture and reheated (stirring until boiling) to thicken.

Test yourself

1. How can sauces be thickened?
2. What ingredients are used to make a blended sauce?
3. What does 'blended' mean?

Roux and all-in-one sauces

Check the facts

The amount of gelatinisation that takes place is affected by the type and the amount of starch used. It is also influenced by the amount of liquid and other ingredients, such as lemon or tomato (the acidity softens the gel).

Roux sauce

Features

Made from **flour** or **cornflour**, **butter** or **margarine**, and **liquid**, such as milk, fish or vegetable stock.

The thickness of the roux depends on the proportion of flour and margarine to the liquid. The roux is made with **equal amounts** of fat and flour. It can have a pouring, coating or binding consistency and is used for white sauces, cheese sauce, fish cakes, lasagne and other pasta dishes.

How to make a roux sauce

Melt the fat, stir in the flour and add the liquid gradually, stirring well. Heat slowly to thicken, stirring all the time.

All-in-one sauce

Features

This is a quicker way to make roux sauce. The features are the same, but it uses a whisk to prevent it going lumpy.

How to make an all-in-one sauce

Put the flour, liquid and fat in a saucepan. Heat slowly, whisking all the time.

Test yourself

1. What ingredients are used for roux and all-in-one sauces?
2. Why should an all-in-one sauce be whisked as it is heated and a roux stirred well?

Check the facts

Nutrition is the study of nutrients and their relationship with food and living things.

Food contains **nutrients**, which are chemical components needed by humans to maintain life and health. The **nutritional value** of a food tells us what nutrients and energy it contains.

The main nutrients which are essential to life are:

- carbohydrate
- fat
- protein
- vitamins
- minerals.

There are two other non-nutrients that are also needed – **water** and **dietary fibre** (or non-starch polysaccharides). Water is necessary because all our body processes depend on water. Dietary fibre is not digested, but it aids digestion by adding bulk to the diet and assisting the removal of waste products in the faeces.

Test yourself

1 What is 'nutrition'?

2 What are 'nutrients'?

3 What are the main nutrients required by the body?

4 Why do we also need water and dietary fibre?

49 Nutrients, sources and functions

nutrients	function	sources
carbohydrate	energy	most foods contain some carbohydrates, e.g. sugar, honey, jam, sweets, chocolate, cakes, biscuits, ice-cream, bread, pasta, potatoes
protein	growth and repair of body	meat, fish, eggs, milk, peas, beans, lentils, soy bean curd, rice, nuts, wheat, corn
fat	energy	butter, margarine, meat, oily fish, egg yolk, cheese, nuts, fried foods, chocolate
fibre (non-starch polysaccharide)	not absorbed by body – needed for healthy digestive system, reduce cholesterol, prevent disease	plant foods
minerals		
calcium	growth and maintenance of teeth and bones	dairy foods (milk, cheese, yoghurt), flour, eggs
iron	essential for formation of red blood cells	red meat, green vegetables, eggs, lentils, bread, dried fruits
phosphorus	strong bones and teeth	present in most protein foods
vitamins		
vitamin A	for vision in dim light, for healthy skin and growth	dairy foods, eggs, margarine, green and yellow vegetables **retinol**: animal foods and **carotene**: plant foods
thiamin (B1)	transfer of energy from carbohydrate	bread, cereals, potatoes, milk
riboflavin (B2)	transfer of energy from protein, fat, carbohydrate	milk, meat, cereals, eggs
niacin (B)	release of energy from foods	meat, meat products, potatoes, cereals
B12	formation of red blood cells	liver, meat, meat products, milk
folate/folic acid (B)	formation of red blood cells and shown to reduce the risk of neural tube defects e.g. spina bifida.	not present in foods and can only be taken by supplement some bread and cereals are fortified with folic acid
vitamin C	healthy skin, absorption of iron	fruit and vegetables
vitamin D	growth and maintenance of strong bones and teeth, absorption of calcium	made by the body when skin is exposed to sunlight

Check the facts

No one food contains all the required nutrients so a variety of foods must be eaten. Healthy eating is about making sure that you eat the right combinations of a variety of foods to provide the nutrients necessary for well-being.

The Balance of Good Health

To help people understand about healthy eating, a scheme called *The Balance of Good Health* (1994) was produced. This uses a diagram of a dinner plate to show the proportions of the different basic food groups that people are advised to eat. The key message is that healthy eating can be achieved over time if you use the plate as a guide to choosing foods. It is what you eat over a period of time, rather than on any one particular day, that will affect future health.

Test yourself

1 What is *The Balance of Good Health*?

2 What is meant by 'healthy eating'?

51 Food groups and choices

five food groups	bread, cereals and potatoes	fruits and vegetables	milk and dairy foods	meat, fish and alternatives	fatty and sugary foods
types of foods	all types of bread, rolls, crackers, rice cakes, naan bread; all types of grains (oats, barley, rye, couscous), breakfast cereals, pasta, rice, noodles, beans and lentils	fresh, frozen and canned fruit and vegetables; dried fruit, fruit juice, beans and lentils	milk, cheese, yoghurt, fromage frais	meat, poultry, fish, eggs, nuts, seeds, beans, lentils, bacon, salami, meat products, beefburgers, canned beans, fish fingers, canned fish, fish cakes, frozen fish	margarine, low-fat spread, butter, ghee, cooking oils, oily salad dressing, cream, chocolate, crisps, biscuits, sweets, sugar, fizzy drinks, puddings
main nutrients	carbohydrates, fibre, calcium, iron, B vitamins	vitamin C, carotenes, iron, calcium, folate, fibre, some carbohydrate	calcium, protein, vitamins B, A and D	iron, protein, B vitamins, zinc, magnesium	some vitamins and essential fatty acids; a lot of fat, salt and sugar
how much to choose	eat lots	eat lots; try to have five servings each day	eat moderate amounts; choose low-fat versions	eat moderate amounts, choose low-fat versions	eat sparingly – small amounts, not too often
what types to choose	wholemeal, wholegrain, high-fibre versions, try not to fry too often (e.g. chips) or add too much fat (spreading butter, or adding sauces)	eat a wide variety; avoid adding fatty or sugary, rich sauces	lower-fat versions, including semi-skimmed milk, low-fat yoghurt, low-fat cheese	lower-fat versions, cut fat off meat, have poultry without the skin, fish without batter	keep to small amounts; should not replace food in the four main groups

Check the facts

Expert committees research and provide advice on what we should think about when planning our diets.

The Ministry of Agriculture, Fisheries and Food (MAFF) has produced eight guidelines for a balanced diet:

1. enjoy your food
2. eat a variety of different foods
3. eat the right amount to be a healthy weight for your height
4. eat plenty of foods rich in starch and fibre
5. don't eat too much fat
6. don't eat sugary foods too often
7. store and prepare foods carefully so that their vitamins and minerals are not lost
8. if you drink alcohol, keep within sensible limits.

Eating the right balance of a wide range of foods will provide most people with all the energy and nutrients they need, in the correct proportions. A balanced diet, together with regular physical activity, can help people maintain a healthy body weight and may reduce their chance of developing diet-related illnesses, such as heart disease.

Achieving a balanced diet will depend on many factors so it is not helpful to prescribe one type of diet. Individuals need different amounts of energy and nutrients, and many other factors affect what a person chooses to eat, such as cost, religion, availability, likes and dislikes.

Test yourself

1 What are the **eight** guidelines for healthy eating?

2 Why are a balanced diet and regular physical exercise important?

Saving Lives: Our Healthier Nation

Check the facts

Saving Lives: Our Healthier Nation (1999) is an action plan to tackle poor health in England. There are similar strategies for Scotland and Wales.

This action plan seeks to improve the health of everyone and, in particular, those worst off. It is estimated that if these targets are met, up to 300 000 untimely and unnecessary deaths will be prevented.

The four main priorities identified in England are:

1 **Cancer**
To reduce the death rate from cancer in people under 75 years by at least a fifth by 2010 – saving up to 100 000 lives in total.

Cancer still affects almost every family in Britain at some time. Around two in five people develop cancer during their lifetime and one in four people die from it. Not all cancers are preventable but many are by tackling factors, such as diet, smoking or the environments which cause them.

2 **Coronary heart disease and stroke**
To reduce the death rate from coronary heart disease (CHD), strokes and related diseases in people under 75 years by at least two fifths by 2010 – saving up to 200 000 lives in total.

Coronary heart disease) strokes and related conditions are a major cause of early death, accounting for about 66 000 deaths each year in people aged under 75, a third of all deaths in men (18 000 deaths) and one fifth of all deaths in women (7000 deaths) aged under 65 years.

Heart diseases and strokes can be prevented by tackling the risk factors, such as poor diet, smoking and lack of exercise.

3 **Accidents**

4 **Mental health**

Test yourself

1 What is *Saving Lives: Our Healthier Nation*?

2 What are the **four** main priorities for England?

3 What are the risk factors for cancer, heart disease and strokes?

Check the facts

Dietary guidelines include standards, advice and information about nutritional needs and nutrient intakes. Manufacturers refer to these when developing food products.

Dietary Reference Values (DRVs) give an indication of the nutritional requirements of different people who are in good health. They give several figures to cover the needs of most healthy people in the population and recognise that, even within one group, some people will have higher or lower requirements than others. Two DRVs which are commonly used are **Reference Nutrient Intake** (RNI) and **Estimated Average Requirements** (EARs).

RNI is the amount of nutrients (**protein**, **vitamins** and **minerals**) that is thought to cover the needs of almost everyone in a particular group.

EARs are the DRVs used for **energy**.

Lower Reference Nutrient Intake is the amount of a nutrient required by a very small proportion of the population who have particularly low needs.

Safe intake is the term used to indicate an amount of a nutrient that is enough for almost everyone but not so large as to cause undesired effects.

	estimated average requirements for energy in kJ (kcal)	
age (years)	**male**	**female**
7–10	8274 (1970)	7380 (1740)
11–14	9324 (2220)	7749 (1845)
15–18	11 571 (2755)	8862 (2110)
19–50	10 710 (2550)	8148 (1940)
51–59	10 710 (2550)	7980 (1900)
60–64	9996 (2380)	7980 (1900)
65–74	9786 (2330)	7980 (1900)
75+	8820 (2100)	7602 (1810)
pregnancy (last 3 months)		need an extra 840 (200)
breastfeeding 1 month		need an extra 1890 (450)

Test yourself

1 What is meant by 'DRVs'?

2 What is meant by 'RNIs'?

3 What is meant by 'EARs'?

Nutrition throughout life

Check the facts

People's nutritional needs change throughout their lives.

- **Childhood** is a period of rapid growth and development when nutritional needs are high.
- **Men and women** tend to have different nutritional and energy needs because of physical differences between them.
- **Physically-active** people will have higher energy needs than those people who are less active. Nutritional requirements will reflect these general differences.

In addition, there are people who may have **special dietary needs**.

Examples of such special dietary needs include:
- vegetarians
- weight loss
- people with allergies or food intolerances, for example, intolerance to milk (lactose) or wheat (gluten).

Test yourself

1 Why do people's nutritional needs change throughout their lives or differ from other people's?

2 Name **one** special dietary need and explain what a person with that need is unable to eat.

Check the facts

Computer software programs can provide detailed and accurate information about the nutritional content of foods.

You can use computer software to calculate the nutritional content of specific foods, recipes, dishes or products.

You will first need to enter data, such as amounts, weights or portion sizes and the foods you want to analyse. The computer will then provide data in the form of a **nutritional breakdown** or **profile**.

Once you have this information, you can use the computer to produce it in the form of a chart or graph. You can also manipulate and alter ratios and proportions of a recipe. For some purposes, a visual representation of the data is more useful than raw figures.

nutritional information	product 1	product 2
typical values	**100 g provides**	**100 g provides**
energy	1664 Kj/390 Kcal	1825 Kj/438 Kcal
protein	7.3 g	11.2 g
carbohydrate	28.1 g	30.4 g
fat	25.7 g	30.2 g
fibre	1.5 g	1.5 g
sodium	0.6 g	0.8 g

Test yourself

1 Why is a computer used for nutritional analysis?

Check the facts

Meat is muscle tissue from animals.

Meat is made up from long, thin muscle fibres. These are bound together in bundles by thin sheets of connective tissue.

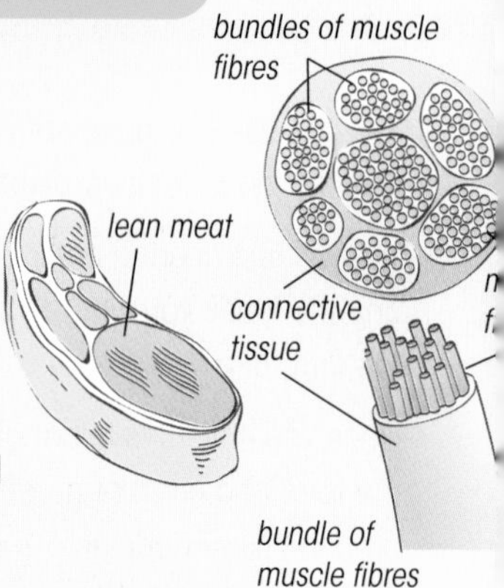

Connective tissue is made from basic proteins: **collagen**, **elastin** and **reticulin**. Collagen is weakened by heat and forms gelatin, which is soluble. This change helps the meat to become tender. The two other proteins are not weakened by heat, yet provide elasticity and strength.

types of meat	example
beef/veal	rump steak, brisket, loin of veal
lamb/mutton	chops, shoulder, shank
pork/bacon	chops, gammon steak, spare ribs
poultry	chicken, duck, goose
offal	liver, kidney, tripe
game	pheasant, rabbit

Tenderness

Some varieties of meat are tough and can be hard to cut or chew. This may be due to the **type of animal**, its **age**, level of **activity** and the **part of the animal** being eaten. Tenderness can be improved by **reducing the length of muscle fibre**, by mincing, hitting it with a tenderising hammer or using meat tenderizers that contain **proteolytic enzymes** that digest muscle fibre and connective tissue. Tenderness can be improved by marinading in wine or lemon juice and by using a moist method of cooking, such as casseroling.

Colour

Muscles used for physical activity contain large quantities of the pigment, **myoglobin**, and are therefore darker in colour. For example, in poultry the legs and wings, which do the most work, tend to be darker and tougher.

Test yourself

1 What is meat?

2 Why is meat cooked?

3 How can meat be tenderised?

Check the facts

Meat analogues are meat-like products that mimic the sensory qualities of meat, for example, textured vegetable protein (TVP).

Some people choose not to eat meat for a variety of reasons and obtain all their protein from other sources. Meat analogues may be used to add bulk to, or extend, food products, e.g. TVP may be used to reduce the cost of a product, such as chilli con carne.

Textured Vegetable Protein (TVP)

Globular soya protein is unfolded to form bundles of short fibres of extended chains of protein.
It has a beany taste that needs to be flavoured.
Dried TVP should be kept cool, in an air-tight container away from direct sunlight. It can be used plain, flavoured, minced or in lumps for sausages, burgers, pasta dishes, etc.

Myco-protein

Fermenting *Fusarium graminearium* produces fine fibres, which form together to make myco-protein.
It has a similar texture to meat and contains a small amount of fibre.
Myco-protein should be kept in a refrigerator or freezer until needed.
Quorn™ is an example of a myco-protein and can be used minced, in lumps, formed for savoury sauces, and in pies and pasties.

Tofu

Soya beans are ground and sieved. The proteins coagulate, producing a soft, cheese-like product.
Tofu is semi-solid and absorbs flavours well but doesn't have a meaty texture.
Tofu should be kept in a refrigerator or freezer unit until needed. It can be used plain or smoked for sausages, burgers and pasta dishes.

Tempeh

Tempeh is made from fermented soya beans.
It is solid, has a white fluffy outer layer and can be sliced, used in stir fries or steamed.
Tempeh should be kept in a refrigerator or freezer unit until needed.

Test yourself

1 Name **four** meat analogues and describe how they are used.

2 Which meat analogues are made from soya?

3 What is 'myco-protein'?

Check the facts

Fish has a muscle composition similar to that of meat but has far less connective tissue and is, therefore, more tender and quicker to cook.

Fish muscle is made from segments of short fibres, which give the characteristic flaky texture. These segments are separated by sheets of fine connective tissue, which is very fragile and easily converted to gelatine. The combination of short muscle fibres and gelatin gives fish its tenderness. This is why overcooking will result in fish falling apart.

Types

Fish can be grouped according to its origin (fresh water or sea water) or its fat content and type (oily fish, white fish, shellfish).

Fresh water: e.g. salmon, trout

Sea water **Pelagic**: these swim near to the surface of the sea, e.g. herring, mackerel, sprat and sardine.
Demersal: these swim close to the sea bed, e.g. cod, haddock, plaice and sole.
Shellfish molluscs: e.g. cockles, winkles and mussels.
Crustaceans: e.g. lobster, scampi, prawn and crab.

Characteristics

Fat content

Oily fish have more than 5 % fat in their flesh, e.g. sardine and salmon. White fish have less than 5 % fat in their flesh, e.g. cod and halibut.

Tenderness

Fish muscle is composed of short segments of fibres that are easily broken. Care needs to be taken in preparation and cooking.

Preservation

Fish start to deteriorate as soon as they are caught. Most fish are put on ice or frozen to halt this process. This increases their shelf-life. They can also be prepared and then frozen, salted, marinaded, smoked, canned and sun-dried to increase shelf-life.

Test yourself

1 Why is fish more tender and quicker to cook than meat?

2 How can fish be grouped?

Check the facts

Eggs have been used as a food for centuries and have many uses in food products.

In the UK, hens' eggs are the most commonly eaten type of eggs. The eggs are graded by size and quality, according to **European Union regulations**. There are four main systems of egg production: **battery farming** (intensive), **deep litter** (semi-intensive), **barn** and **free range**.

Composition

An egg is made up from three main parts: the **shell**, **white** and **yolk**.

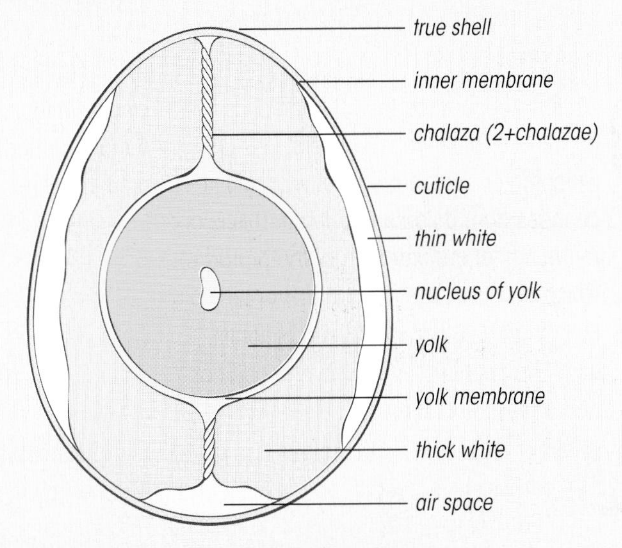

As an egg gets older, several changes occur:

- water moves from the white to the yolk
- the yolk structure weakens
- the egg white becomes thinner
- the air space increases
- bacteria may enter through the shell
- a bad egg smell occurs due to the production of hydrogen sulphide and related compounds.

Test yourself

1 Name **four** systems for producing eggs.

2 What are the main parts of an egg?

3 What happens when an egg gets older?

Milk and milk products

Check the facts

Most milk undergoes some form of heat processing, e.g. pasteurisation, sterilisation or ultra-high temperature (UHT) treatment, to ensure that harmful micro-organisms are destroyed before consumption and to improve keeping qualities.

Cows' milk is the most commonly consumed type of milk in the UK.

product	composition	uses
milk	An emulsion – a suspension of tiny fat droplets in water.	fresh cows' milk (whole, semi-skimmed, skimmed), goats', ewes', dried, UHT, condensed
cream	Made by separating the fat and solids from milk. It is a fat-in-water emulsion. When whipping or double cream is whipped, it changes from a liquid to a foam. This is due to the partial denaturation of the proteins, which stabilises the mixture by trapping air.	single, whipping, double, clotted, sour, crème fraîche
yoghurt	Milk is coagulated and soured by lactic acid. The acid is produced by the addition of harmless bacteria.	Greek, bio, set, natural, flavoured
cheese	An enzyme called rennin is used to clot the milk and produce the milk solids (casein curd) and liquid (whey),which is drained off. Some cheeses are then pressed and ripened. The different kinds of cheese result from different methods of production and raw ingredients.	Brie, Gouda, Stilton, Cheddar, cottage, Ricotta
butter	Water-in-oil emulsion made from cream.	unsalted, salted, flavoured, e.g. garlic

Test yourself

1 Name **four** milk products.

2 How is cheese made?

3 Name **four** different cheeses.

Check the facts

All cereals are members of the grass family. Cereals are also known as staple foods as they often make up the bulk of the diet since they are relatively cheap to produce.

Each cereal has unique properties that make it suitable for a variety of food products. Cereals require different conditions to grow, e.g. rice is grown in damp, tropical climates, such as India and China.

Rye

Rye contains little gluten, so produces low volume, dense breads.
Primary processing produces grains and flour.
Thickening agent (gelatinisation).

Barley

Barley is sold as pearl barley – the whole grain with its husk removed.
Primary processing produces grains (pearl barley) and malt.
Pearl barley may also be used to thicken a soup or casserole.

Wheat

Usually ground into flour for a wide range of products.Type of flour differs due to the extraction rate.
Primarily processed into grains, cous cous and flour. It is the most commonly used cereal in the UK.
Thickening agent (gelatinisation).

Oats

Oats are rolled rather than crushed into coarse, medium and fine grades of oatmeal.
Primary processing produces grains, flour, rolled oats and oatmeal.

Maize

May be milled like wheat.
Germ is refined to produce corn oil.
Primary processing produces whole grains, flour and oil.
Thickening agent (gelatinisation).

Rice

The outer husk is removed from brown rice and white rice is milled and polished further to remove the bran and germ.
Rice is categorised by size, shape and where it is grown.
Primary processing produces grains (white or brown) and flour.
Thickening agent (gelatinisation).
Rice flour can thicken acidic sauces as it is resistant to effects of low pH.
It is sometimes used to bulk a food product, e.g. vegetarian burgers.

Test yourself

1 What are cereals?

2 What is meant by 'staple' foods?

3 Name **six** cereals.

Check the facts

Wheat flour is sold as wholemeal, brown or white. Milling and processing wheat grains affect the sensory, functional and nutritional properties of the flour.

- Wholemeal flour uses the whole grain; nothing is removed during milling.
- White flour is refined, separating it from the bran, (extraction rate: ~75 %).
- Brown flour contains some bran.

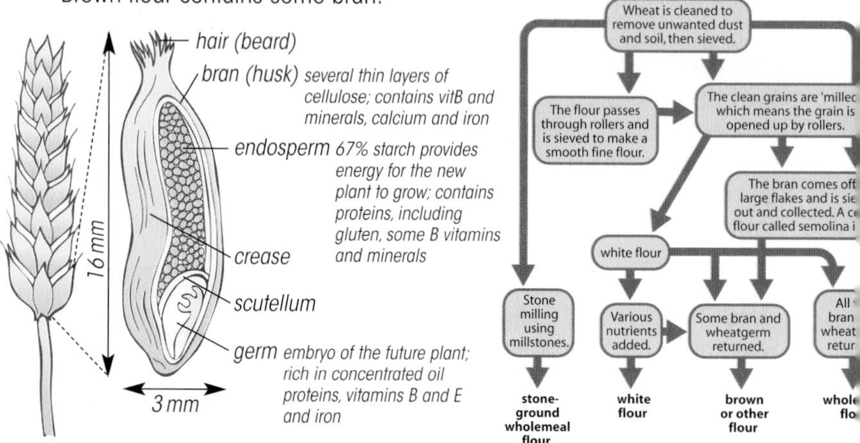

UK law requires brown and white flour to be fortified with nutrients that may have been lost during milling.

The amount and type of protein in flour affects the final product:

1 **Strong flour** is used for bread; and flaky, puff and choux pastry. It is made from a variety of wheat with a high (17 %) protein content. The proteins (**gliadin** and **glutenin**) help develop the characteristic structure of bread. When water is added to flour, the proteins hydrate to form **gluten**, which is a strong, elastic substance that forms a network throughout the dough. Fat and sugar inhibit gluten development, but salt and ascorbic acid aid it.

2 **Soft flour** is produced from a different variety of wheat. It has a lower protein content (8 %) and is mixed with fat to produce a crumbly and light texture, mainly used for making cakes, shortcrust pastry and biscuits.

Test yourself

1 What is the difference between wholemeal and white flour?
2 What is the difference between strong and soft flour?
3 What inhibits gluten development
4 What promotes gluten development?

Check the facts

Fats and oils have the same chemical structure. Fats which are liquid at room temperature are called oils.

Edible fats and oils are obtained from both animals and plants. The main animal sources are **milk** (butter, ghee and cream), **meat** (dripping, lard and suet) and **marine** (fish oils). The main vegetable sources are **seeds of plants**, such as soya bean, cottonseed, groundnut, palm, linseed, olive, sesame and corn. The oils are extracted from the cells of the seeds.

Animal fats contain mainly saturated fatty acids

Butter is not a pure fat, but an emulsion of water in oil. It is mostly used for spreading, cakes, biscuits, sauces and pastry.

Lard comes from pig fat. Its plasticity makes it a good shortening ingredient and is often used for pastry, frying and roasting.

Suet is the fat around the organs of animals, e.g. ox and sheep. It is very solid and hard, and is used for suet pudding, dumplings and jam roly poly.

Vegetable fats contain high levels of unsaturated fatty acids

Sunflower, **soya**, **olive** and **corn oil** usually contain natural antioxidants, which resist rancidity. They are used in margarine, salad dressings and for frying.

Margarine is a solid emulsion of water in oil. It is available as:

- blocks – good for products that require the fat to be rubbed-in
- soft – good for cakes, pastry and spreading on bread
- low-fat spread – very low-fat spreads are unsuitable for frying and baking due to their high water content.

Sometimes a blend of fats is used in a product to take advantage of the desirable characteristics of several types of fat.

Fish oils contain a high percentage of unsaturated fatty acids

Fish oils are normally hydrogenated (hardened). They are rich in vitamins A and D and are used for vitamin supplements and in margarine.

Test yourself

1 What is the difference between fats and oils?

2 Name **two** animal fats and their uses.

3 Name **two** vegetable fats and their uses.

Check the facts

Sugar comes from sugar beet or sugar cane. The sugar is extracted, refined and crystallised into various white and brown forms; to sweeten drinks, for cooking or in food processing.

Sugar, e.g. white table sugar, is a **carbohydrate** consisting of almost pure sucrose. Honey contains many sugars but mainly glucose and fructose. Artificial sweeteners, such as saccharin and aspartame, are also available.

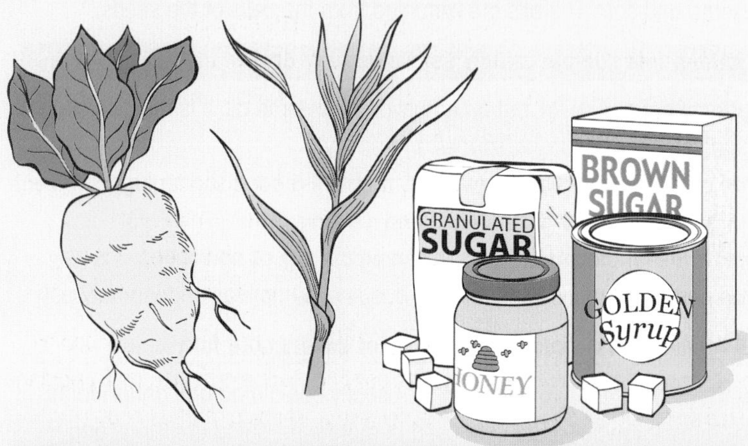

sugar	uses
granulated	hot drinks, mincemeat filling, cakes, sauces, macaroons, jam, ice cream, soft drinks, chutney
demerara	fruit crumble topping, rich fruit cake
icing sugar	royal icing, fondant icing
caster	cakes, swiss roll, meringue, shortbread, fruit pie filling, syrup
soft brown	Dundee cake and other bakery items, fudge
honey	cakes, flapjacks, cereals
golden syrup	flapjacks, tarts
treacle	rich fruit cakes, spicy sauces

Test yourself

1 Where does sugar come from?

2 Name **four** different types of sugar and what they are used for.

Check the facts

The edible parts of fruit and vegetables are made from similar types of cells.

The cell has an outer wall, made mostly of **cellulose**. Within the cell there is a jelly-like substance, called **cytoplasm**, which carries **fat droplets** and colour **pigments**. In potatoes and yams, **starch** is also carried in cytoplasm.

The major part of the cell, the **vacuole**, contains **cell sap**. The sap is watery and contains **sugar**, **pigments** and **salts**. Between the cells are small pockets known as **intercellular air spaces**, which give raw fruits and vegetables their opaqueness. On cooking, the cell structure breaks down so raw fruits and vegetables become softer.

The acidic nature of fruit and vegetables acts as natural protection against spoilage by micro-organisms. Fruit has a higher sugar content than vegetables, which makes them susceptible to mould. Fruit ripens and vegetables mature on storage, changing flavour, appearance and texture.

Freshly cut fruit discolours by oxidation – this is **enzymic browning**. It can be slowed down by blanching to denature enzymes, using antioxidants, by adding an acidic or sugary solution to the surface or by keeping the fruit cool.

Some fruits, e.g. apples, are a rich source of **pectin**, which is used to set jam.

types of fruits	**soft fruits**	raspberry, blackberry, redcurrant, strawberry, bilberry
	fleshy	apple, papaya, pineapple, pear, banana
	citrus	orange, lime, lemon, kumquat, grapefruit
	vine	grape, water melon, cantaloupe
	stone	plum, apricot, peach, lychee, cherry, mango
types of vegetables	**bulbs**	onion, garlic, shallot, leek
	roots	beetroot, swede, salsify, carrot, parsnip, radish
	fruits	aubergine, marrow, plantain, tomato
	tubers	potato, sweetpotato, yam, cassava, jerusalem artichoke
	flowers	broccoli, cauliflower, calabrese
	leaves	spinach, cabbage, parsley, endive, lettuce, watercress
	stem	asparagus, fennel, celery
	fungi	oyster and button mushroom
	pulses	pea, bean, lentil

Test yourself

1 Name **four** different types of fruit and **four** different types of vegetables.

2 Describe the cellular structure of fruit and vegetables.

3 Why do fruits discolour when cut. How could you prevent this?

Heat exchange

Check the facts

As a food is heated, its molecules absorb energy and vibrate more vigorously. The faster they move, the more the temperature of the food rises. If heat is removed, the molecules become less active, reducing the food's temperature.

The transfer of heat to, or from, particular foods is important in both domestic food preparation and industrial food manufacture.

Application of heat – e.g. cooking

Applying heat in the preparation of a food or mixture of foods may:

- improve appearance, taste, smell and texture
- prevent spoilage and increase keeping qualities
- destroy bacteria
- improve digestibility.

Removal of heat – e.g. chilling and freezing

The removal of heat (cooling) from foods may:

- modify appearance and texture, e.g. formation of ice crystals
- prevent spoilage and increase keeping qualities, i.e. retards growth of micro-organisms
- aid processing, e.g. tempering meat before slicing.

Methods of heat exchange

- Conduction, e.g. stir frying with a wok, production of ice cream.
- Convection, e.g. boiling, blast chilling.
- Radiation, e.g. grilling, microwaving, sun drying.

All of these methods are used in the application, or removal of, heat from a food product. One method or several may be in action at any time, depending on the food and the time and equipment available.

Test yourself

1 Why is heat applied to food?

2 Why is heat removed from food?

3 Name **three** ways that heat can be exchanged and give an example of each one.

Check the facts

Conduction, convection and radiation are methods of heat exchange.

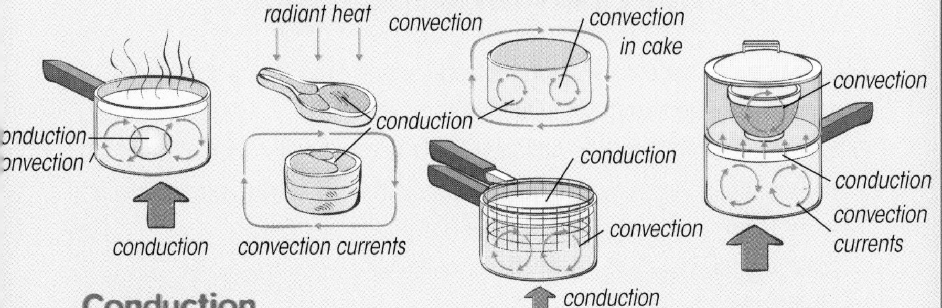

Conduction

Conduction is the exchange of heat by **direct contact** with food on a surface, e.g. stir-frying vegetables in a wok, pasteurising milk in a plate heat-exchanger or making ice cream.

Convection

Convection is the exchange of heat by the **application of a gas or liquid current**, e.g. boiling potatoes in hot water, frying, baking bread, or blasting cold air through peas to freeze them.

The processes of convection and conduction may work together in order to exchange heat. For example, first the surface of a baked potato is heated by convection then the heat is conducted through to the centre of the potato.

Radiation

Radiation is energy in the form of **rays**. The rays pass through the air until they come into contact with the food; some are absorbed while others are reflected. Sun drying is a traditional method of using the sun's rays to preserve food.

Grilling involves the use of **infra-red heat rays** created by gas flames, charcoal or glowing electric elements.

Microwaves are **electromagnetic radiations** of high energy and short wavelengths. They quickly heat anything containing water, by causing the water present to oscillate (i.e. vibrate) which produces heat.

Test yourself

1 What is 'conduction'?

2 What is 'convection'?

3 What is 'radiation'?

Food hygiene

Check the facts

The *General Food Hygiene Regulations* (1995) implemented in the UK ensure common food hygiene rules across the European Union.

Food hygiene is necessary to produce and supply food that is safe to eat. This involves more than just cleanliness:

- protecting food from contamination by micro-organisms, foreign bodies or chemicals
- reducing the number of micro-organisms in food or preventing any from multiplying
- destroying harmful micro-organisms in food.

Bacteria

What are bacteria?

Bacteria are tiny, living organisms that can't be seen with the naked eye. Most bacteria are harmless but a few (pathogens) may cause illness, such as food poisoning. When pathogens are present in food, they can't be seen and don't cause any changes to the taste, smell or appearance of food.

Where do pathogens come from?

- **People**: on skin, in noses, mouths, ears and hair and sometimes in the gut.
- **Animals**: pets, farm animals and pests, such as rats, mice and insects.
- **Raw foods**: raw poultry, meat and eggs and raw vegetables.
- **Food waste** and **rubbish**.

How do bacteria grow?

Most pathogens must multiply to high numbers in food in order to cause illness. They multiply by **binary fission**, where one cell divides into two. In order to grow and multiply, pathogens need:

- **food** – pathogens generally grow in protein foods, e.g. poultry, meat, eggs, fish and dairy products; one exception is a pathogen which grows in rice
- **moisture** – bacteria need moisture in order to grow
- **warmth** – pathogens multiply rapidly at temperatures around 37 °C but will grow in a temperature range of 5–63 °C
- **time** – bacteria multiplies rapidly in favourable conditions.

Test yourself

1 What are 'pathogens'?

2 Where do pathogens come from?

3 What conditions do pathogens need to multiply?

Check the facts

Food poisoning is commonly caused by the presence of harmful bacteria (pathogens) or the toxins (poisons) they produce, when eaten in food.

There are thousands of cases of food poisoning each year. The most common symptoms of food poisoning are feeling and being sick, diarrhoea and stomach pains. Symptoms may develop as rapidly as one hour after eating affected food but usually take several hours or even a few days to develop. Illness usually lasts between 24 hours and a few days but can affect some people, particularly babies and older people, more severely. Occasionally food poisoning can be fatal.

What do people do wrong?
• Preparing food too far in advance
• Storing food at room temperature
• Inadequate thawing, cooling or reheating
• Undercooking
• Eating raw food
• Keeping food warm (below 63 °C)
• Infected food handlers
• Contaminated processed food
• Poor hygiene

Test yourself

1 What are the symptoms of food poisoning?

2 What are the main causes of food poisoning?

Food poisoning bacteria

Check the facts

Campylobacter • Meat and poultry.
Symptoms: onset 2–11 days. Fever, headache and dizziness for a few hours, then abdominal pain. Lasts 2–7 days; can recur over a few weeks.

Clostridium botulinum • Canned meat due to inadequate processing and in vegetables and fish when they are canned incorrectly.
Symptoms: onset 24–72 hours. Voice change, double vision, drooping eyelids, severe constipation. Death in a week or slow recovery over months.

Clostridium perfringens • Raw meat, cooked meat dishes and poultry.
Symptoms: onset 8–22 hours. Abdominal pain, diarrhoea and nausea. Usually lasts 12–48 hours.

***E. Coli* 0157** • Raw meat and dairy products.
Symptoms: diarrhoea, which may contain blood, can lead to kidney failure, and death.

Listeria monocytogenes • Unpasteurised milk and dairy products, cook-chill foods, paté, meat, poultry and salad vegetables.
Symptoms: mild, flu-like illness, meningitis, septicemia, pneumonia. During pregnancy may lead to miscarriage or birth of an infected baby.

Salmonella • Raw meat, poultry, eggs and raw, unwashed vegetables.
Symptoms: onset 12–36 hours. Headache, aching limbs, fever, abdominal pain, diarrhoea and vomiting. Lasts 1–7 days. Rarely fatal.

Staphylococcus aureus • Meat, dairy products and poultry.
Symptoms: onset 1–6 hours. Severe vomiting, abdominal pain, weakness and lower than normal temperature. Lasts 6–24 hours. The bacteria is often associated with food handlers, so good hygiene practice is essential.

Test yourself

1 Name **three** bacteria responsible for food poisoning.

2 What food poisoning bacteria might be found in unpasteurised milk, cook-chill meals, meat, poultry and salad vegetables?

3 What food poisoning bacteria shows symptoms in humans between 1–6 hours, causing vomiting, abdominal pains, weakness, lower temperature, and lasts for 6–24 hours?

Check the facts

Food poisoning can be prevented by making sure pathogens are not present in food when it is eaten.

How to prevent food poisoning

Controlling contamination of food – make sure that sources of pathogens (i.e. people, pets, etc.) do not have the opportunity to transfer bacteria to food. Wash your hands before touching foods, keep pets out of the kitchen, keep foods covered, make sure that raw foods which may carry pathogens are not allowed to come into contact with foods which are ready to eat.

Preventing growth of bacteria in food – make sure that pathogens, which may be present in foods, are not given the opportunity to grow and multiply. Control the temperature at which foods, particularly those containing protein, are kept, to prevent bacteria from being able to multiply (i.e. either below 5 °C in a refrigerator or freezer or above 63 °C when food has been cooked and is ready to be eaten).

Destroying bacteria in food before it is eaten – make sure that pathogens are destroyed by thorough cooking. Cook food through to centre temperature of 70 °C or above for two minutes in order to kill bacteria. A few pathogens are able to produce spores that protect the bacterial cell, enabling it to survive normal cooking, and become active and multiply again if the food temperature drops back into the growth zone (or danger zone) of 5–63 °C. Cooked food should, therefore, be kept hot above 63 °C or cooled so the food temperature is out of the growth zone, within 1 hour 30 minutes to limit the opportunity for any spores to become active bacteria again.

Test yourself

1 How can you make sure that pathogens do not get transferred to foods?

2 How can you make sure pathogens do not multiply?

3 How can you destroy pathogens before eating food?

Food spoilage and safe storage

Check the facts

As soon as food is harvested, slaughtered or manufactured, it starts to change. Enzymes present in food cause self-destruction. Bacteria, yeasts and moulds can cause microbial spoilage.

Protecting stored food from risk of contamination

- Foods should be wrapped, covered or kept in suitable, clean containers.
- Raw poultry, meat, eggs and fish should be stored separately from ready-to-eat foods. In a refrigerator, for example, it is important to keep raw foods at the bottom of the fridge, and cooked and ready-to-eat items at the top to avoid the risk of blood from meat, cracked egg fluid etc., dripping and transferring pathogens onto other items.
- Raw vegetables, including salad items, may contain pathogens from the soil and should also be kept separate from ready-to-eat foods.
- Storage areas, such as cupboards, refrigerator, freezers etc., should be kept clean.
- Foods should be stored where they are not accessible to pets or pests, e.g. flies, cockroaches, mice or rats.
- Damaged packs of food, where wrapping has been torn or cans badly dented, should be thrown away because they may be contaminated.

Limiting growth of pathogens in stored food

- Foods should be kept out of the temperature zone in which pathogens grow (5–63 °C). Thus, most protein foods need to be kept in a refrigerator or freezer until they are to be prepared for cooking and/or eating.
- The coldest part of the fridge should be should be kept at 0–5 °C and freezers at −18 °C. The operating temperatures of refrigerators and freezers will rise if the door is left open, if hot foods are placed in them for cooling and if they are not defrosted regularly.

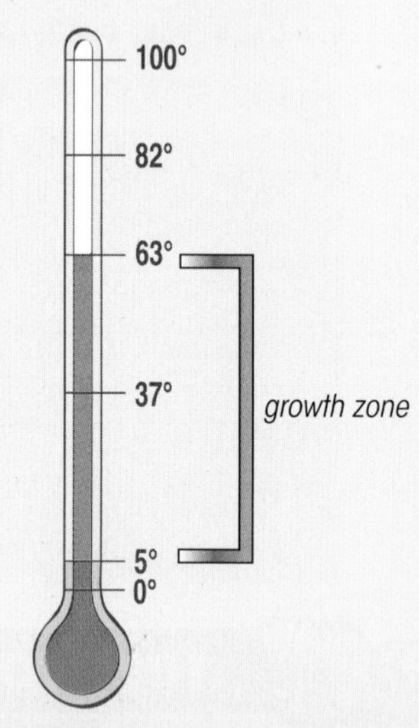

Test yourself

1 Why should raw meat be stored separately from cooked foods?

2 What is the temperature zone in which pathogens grow?

3 Why should you **not** place hot foods in a fridge to cool them?

Check the facts

Safe food handling means protecting food from contamination by pathogens, taking action to limit the growth of pathogens and cooking food thoroughly.

neat and covered hair
clean and tidy clothes
no watch or rings (except a simple wedding ring)
clean hands, short nails and no nail varnish
cuts etc. covered with waterproof dressing
sensible shoes

Protecting food during preparation

- Personal hygiene standards must be met; protective clothing should be worn; hair must be tied back and covered with a hairnet; no rings, jewellery, watches or nail varnish.
- Food preparation should be carried out in an area free from other sources of contamination, e.g. dirty washing, pet bowls, indoor plants.
- Equipment, e.g. work surfaces, chopping boards and knives, must be clean.
- Raw meats and poultry should be prepared separately from other items and all equipment should be washed immediately after use.
- Raw vegetables, including salad items, should be washed before use.
- Ready-to-eat foods must be kept covered and separate from other foods.

Limiting growth of pathogens during preparation

- Foods should not be prepared too far in advance.
- Cold, ready-to-eat foods should be kept in the refrigerator until required.
- Cooked foods should be kept hot (above 63 °C) until they are eaten or cooled down quickly. After cooling, foods should be refrigerated.

Thorough cooking

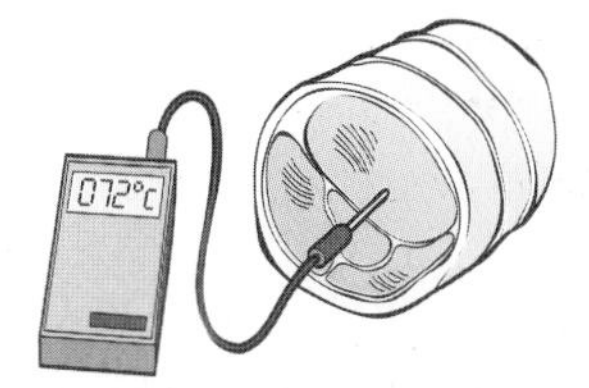

- Frozen foods, particularly joints of meat and poultry, must be thoroughly defrosted before cooking so the heat can penetrate to the centre:
- Most pathogens will be destroyed by cooking to a centre temperature of at 72 °C for at least two minutes. Foods containing meat and poultry should always be cooked thoroughly. Where temperatures can't be checked by a thermometer, it should be ensured that food is piping hot.
- Meat and poultry products, e.g. sausages and chicken, must be checked to make sure the juices are clear and there are no pink bits inside.

Test yourself

1 What is 'personal hygiene'?

2 Why should frozen foods be defrosted before cooking?

3 Why should you use a thermometer to make sure food is piping hot?

Principles of food preservation

Check the facts

The aim of preservation is to prevent food spoilage as a result of growth of micro-organisms and breakdown of food by enzymes.

Micro-organisms, such as yeast, mould and bacteria, cause food to spoil:

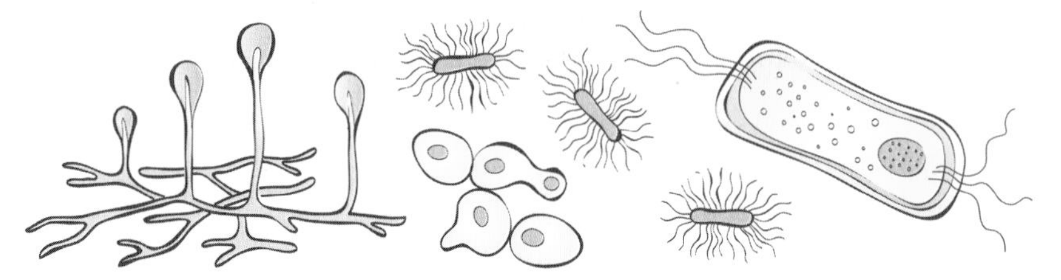

The main methods of food preservation are:

method	principle	example
chill or freeze	retards micro-organism growth and inhibits enzyme activity	frozen vegetables
heat food	destroys micro-organisms and prevents enzyme activity	UHT milk
place in an acidic or alkaline solution	inhibits growth of micro-organisms	pickles
place food in a sugary solution	makes water unavailable to micro-organisms	jam
keep food in an airtight container	deprives micro-organisms of oxygen and prevents further contamination	bottled fruits and canning
reduce the moisture content of the food	makes water, essential for growth, unavailable to micro-organisms	drying herbs, pulses and fruits
fermentation	produces alcohol or acids (e.g. acetic acid or vinegar) to act as preservatives	milk and soy sauce

Test yourself

1 What is 'food preservation'?

2 Name **three** ways of preserving food and give an example for each.

Check the facts

Preservation has been used for thousands of years to keep food through the winter. In the last two centuries, new food processing techniques have been developed.

Smoking

Traditionally, meat and fish were hung over wood fires. This changes the flavour and colour of the food, and increases its keeping qualities.

Bottling

Romans preserved fruit by bottling with honey. Food is packed into glass jars and immersed in acidic, alcoholic, salt or sugar solutions.

Freezing

Freezing was first used in China in 1800 BCE and is now a popular method in many places. It doesn't kill micro-organisms; just retards their growth.

Canning

In 1795, Nicholas Appert put food into bottles (there were no cans then), heated the bottles in water and sealed them. The food kept for a long time.

Sugar preserves

When fruit is boiled with sugar (e.g. jam), the sugar inhibits the growth of micro-organisms by making the water unavailable once enough is evaporated.

Fermentation

Fermented milk was made in India (2000 BCE); beer, wine and bread were made by in Egypt (6000–2000 BCE); and soy sauce has been produced in China for several millennia. During fermentation, alcohol or acids (e.g. acetic acid or vinegar) are produced and act as preservatives.

Salting

Coating food in salt or placing it in a salt solution (brine) reduces the moisture content of the food – it reduces the availability of water. With little moisture, micro-organism growth is retarded.

Pickling

Fruit and vegetables are covered with vinegar and other ingredients, often including spices. The acidic solution inhibits growth of micro-organisms.

Test yourself

1 Why were foods preserved many years ago?

2 How are foods smoked traditionally?

3 Who discovered the canning process?

Pasteurisation

Check the facts

Pasteurisation is a form of heat processing, which increases the shelf-life of food. The heat kills most of the micro-organisms that cause food spoilage and disease.

The two main types of industrial pasteurisation are:

- **batch pasteurisation** – the product is held at a specific temperature for a long time, e.g. 62–63 °C for 30–35 minutes.

- **high-temperature, short time or HTST pasteurisation** – the product is heated to a higher temperature but for a shorter time, e.g. 72 °C for 15 seconds for milk using a plate heat exchanger. After the milk has been heated it is passed through a regenerator, which brings it into close contact with the cold, raw milk pipe. The heat is recycled as the cold, raw milk is warmed by close contact with the heated milk, which is, in turn, cooled.

Pasteurisation only destroys pathogenic bacteria and, therefore, pasteurised products will only last a few days in the fridge, whereas other processing methods destroy all bacteria and can be stored for long periods of time at room temperature. However, the tasting quality is not as good as that achieved by pasterusation.

The time, temperature and pasteurisation methods used differ according to the product being pasteurised. This minimises the chemical and physical changes that effect the flavour and colour.

The time and temperature will depend on:

- food type
- viscosity (thickness or lumpiness) of the product
- pH of the product
- particle size
- equipment used
- method used.

Test yourself

1 What is 'pasteurisation'?

2 What are the **two** types of industrial pasteurisation?

Check the facts

Sterilisation is a severe form of heat processing that destroys most micro-organisms. The flavour and appearance of a food product may change during sterilisation.

Processing

Sterilisation uses temperatures exceeding 100 °C to destroy most micro-organisms present in a food. This is important as some micro-organisms can form spores that have the ability to survive at high temperatures. If the correct temperature is not reached, there is the possibility that the spores will germinate and grow and could result in food poisoning. Some organisms can survive the sterilisation process if not processed for enough time or at a high enough temperature, e.g. *Clostridium botulinum*. The time and temperature chosen will depend upon the:

- micro-organisms present
- properties of the food product
- product's initial temperature
- pH of the product
- microbe count
- size/volume of the container, e.g. can.

Packaging

The product is packaged in air-tight containers before or after heat treatment.

If the product is packaged before processing, the containers must be made of materials that will not be affected by heat, e.g. cans, glass bottles, foil parcels, plastics and special laminates. They must also be completely air tight to avoid re-contamination.

If packaging follows heating, the containers must be sterilised before use and filled under aseptic conditions.

Test yourself

1 What is 'sterilisation'?

2 Why are temperatures over 100 °C used?

Check the facts

Ultra-heat treatment (UHT) is a process where the food is heated to a very high temperature for a short time.

The UHT process was developed to kill or retard all micro-organisms without changing the flavour or appearance of the food as much as sterilisation does.

UHT is a continuous process and after sterilisation the product is packaged into sterile containers. Typical temperatures and times specified for UHT treatment of milk are 130–150 °C for 1–3 seconds.

As the product is moving continuously, rather than being stationary, high temperatures can be reached. This results in fewer chemical changes, such as non-enzymic browning due to caramelisation, but the same sterilising effect is achieved.

For example, when milk is UHT-processed, there is an increased retention of:

- nutrients, due to short time
- colour, as there is no caramelisation of milk sugars
- flavour, as there is no caramelisation of milk sugars
- texture, since there is no denaturing of proteins.

Test yourself

1 What does UHT stand for?

2 Why was this process developed?

Check the facts

Canning destroys all micro-organisms, and their spores, by heating. It involves sterilising food in air-tight containers to prevent re-contamination.

The stages of canning are:

- washing and preparing the food, e.g. peeling, chopping
- blanching fruit or vegetables, i.e. immersing in boiling water
- filling the cans
- sealing the cans
- heating in a retort (see below)
- cooling
- labelling with 'best before' date.

Filling

The cans are filled automatically with a measured weight or volume of product. A solution of brine, savoury sauce, fruit juice or sugar syrup is usually added. Food is also packaged in plastic containers, for example, ambient ready meals. These are known as 'plastic cans'.

Sealing

The cans are sealed under a vacuum, using a double seam on the can rim. A vacuum is applied to draw out the air at the top of the can and seal the lid.

Heating in a retort

Batches of cans are placed in a retort, which works like a large pressure cooker. Canning is quicker under pressure, as the temperature rises to 121 °C. **Solid pack** contents, e.g. canned meat, need more time as the heat needs to penetrate the product by conduction. However, **liquid pack** contents, e.g. soups, need far less time as the liquid present helps transfer the heat by convection.

Cooling

The cans are cooled using cool water sprays and cooling tanks to prevent overcooking.

Test yourself

1 Name **two** products that are canned.

2 List the main stages of canning.

3 What is a 'retort'?

Dehydration

Check the facts

Dehydration is the removal of most of the water from foods. It doesn't kill micro-organisms, but stops their growth by making water unavailable to them; increasing a product's shelf-life.

Micro-organisms need water in order to grow and reproduce. Dehydration reduces the water activity level, weight and bulk of the food and helps to preserve the product.

There are different dehydration techniques suitable for a specific range of foods. Many products, such as vegetables, are diced before drying, to increase their surface area and make water loss more rapid. Blanching may be necessary to inactivate enzymes that cause browning.

Spray drying, e.g. coffee powder, dried milk.

A fine, liquid spray is injected into a hot air blast in a chamber. The water evaporates in seconds, leaving behind the solid part of the product in a powdered form. This powder is usually too fine to disperse in water, so a little moisture is added to make it clump together in larger particles. This improves the 'wetability' of the product and helps it dissolve when added to water. Fluidised bed drying is used to granulate these types of powders.

Fluidised bed drying, e.g. peas, coffee.

Warm air is blown upwards, directly underneath the food, causing it to flow and remain separated.

Tunnel drying, e.g. vegetables.

Hot air is blown over the product.

Roller drying, e.g. instant mashed potato, baby foods.

The food product, in a liquid or paste form, is uniformly spread over heated rollers or drums, which rotate slowly. The heat causes the moisture to evaporate leaving behind a dried product. A scraper then removes this.

Sun drying, e.g. sun-dried raisins, fish.

A traditional method of drying. Slow and only practical in hot, dry climates.

Test yourself

1 Why does dehydration stop the growth of micro-organisms?

2 List **four** foods that can be dehydrated.

3 Name **three** ways that foods can be dehydrated?

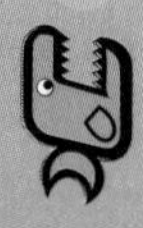

Check the facts

When frozen, the very low temperatures inhibit the growth of micro-organisms and slow down enzyme activity. The ice crystals make water in food unavailable to micro-organisms and prevent their growth.

There are many methods of freezing food, including:

Immersion freezing – immersing foods in ice.

Traditionally, foods were immersed in solutions of salt and ice, e.g. brine freezing of fish at sea. Refrigerants are now sprayed directly onto the food.

Plate freezing – pressing food between two refrigerated plates.

The food is prepared then packed between flat, hollow, refrigerated metal plates that press tightly on the food. It is a good technique for blocks, such as fish for fish fingers.

Blast freezing – blasting a stream of cold air over food.

Batches of food are subjected to a constant stream of cold air (−40 °C or lower) in a tunnel or large cabinet. This is good for irregularly-shaped foods, including those which have already been packaged, e.g. battered cod.

Fluidised bed freezing – the food floats on jets of cold air.

The product (e.g. peas, beans, chopped vegetables or prawns) moves along a conveyor belt. Vertical jets of refrigerated air are blown up through the product, causing it to float and remain separated.

Scraped heat exchange – the food is scraped off a cold surface.

Products, such as ice cream, are frozen like this in order to stir and freeze simultaneously. It reduces large ice crystal formation, producing a smooth end product.

Cryogenic freezing – spraying the food.

Liquid nitrogen or carbon dioxide is sprayed directly onto small food items, such as soft fruits and prawns. Due to the liquids' extremely low temperatures (−196 °C and −78 °C respectively), freezing is almost instant.

Test yourself

1 How does freezing preserve food?

2 Name **three** foods that can be frozen.

3 Name **three** ways of freezing foods.

Check the facts

Chilling is a short-term method of preserving a single food or a mixture of foods, e.g. ready meals. Ready meals require little or no additional preparation.

Chilling is a method of preserving food temporarily. Reducing the temperature slows down the rate of decay.

Cook-chill products

Most food products can be prepared and cooked in advance; then chilled rapidly. They can be stored for a short time before a shopper buys and uses them, and so are very convenient and popular. The food or meal is lightly processed and they taste closer to fresh foods than foods that have been treated by canning or dehydration. There is little loss of flavour, colour, texture, shape or nutritional value.

They have a short shelf-life (usually a few days).

The cook-chill process

Cook-chill products are prepared, cooked and chilled rapidly. They are usually made in batches. They are stored at a temperature just above 0 °C until they are sold. At this temperature, the rate that micro-organisms multiply, and chemical reactions that affect the quality are slowed down.

Examples are: lasagne, cottage pie, chicken tikka masala, pies, pasta and sauce, potato salad.

Test yourself

1 How does chilling preserve food?

2 Name **three** cook-chill products.

3 What is the cook-chill process?

Check the facts

Additives are synthetic or natural substances, added in small quantities to food during processing.

Additives are used to:

- add to product appeal (e.g. glazes, colourings or flavourings)
- prolong shelf life and keep food safe to eat (e.g. sulphur dioxide can be used to prevent sliced apple from browning)
- add additional quality to processed foods (e.g. alginates E401–405 in ice cream help to trap air during freezing, making it lighter and softer).

Additives are coded with E-numbers for classification. This means that, within the European Community, foods containing E-numbers can be moved between countries.

The use of additives is strictly controlled by law. All additives must be cleared for safety, and the permitted amount carefully limited and listed on food labels.

New additives have to pass through many Food Administration Committees before they can lawfully be used commercially.

Test yourself

1 What are E-numbers and where do they come from?

Types of additives

Check the facts

Additives include colours, preservatives, anti-oxidants, emulsifiers and stabilisers.

Colours

Range of E-numbers: E100–199.

Function of E-numbers: add colour or restore colour lost during processing.

Natural example: E160 (e.g. in margarine, pre-packed cheshire cheese).

Synthetic example: E132 (e.g. in sponge pudding, biscuits, sweets).

Preservatives

Range of E-numbers: E200–299.

Function of E-numbers: increase shelf-life by preventing growth of micro-organisms.

Synthetic example: E227 (e.g. in soft drinks, fruit yogurt, processed cheese slices, dried fruit, dehydrated vegetables).

Anti-oxidants

Range of E-numbers: E300–321.

Function of E-numbers: prevent fat-containing food going rancid.

Natural example: E306 (e.g. in packet dessert toppings, vegetable oils).

Synthetic example: E321(e.g. in soft margarine, gravy granules).

Emulsifiers and stabilisers

Range of E-numbers: E322–499.

Function of E-numbers: enable oil and water to form an emulsion and stop them from separating.

Natural example: E322 (e.g. in cheese, condensed milk, dried milk).

Synthetic example: E450 (e.g. in chocolate, powdered milk, dessert mixes).

Test yourself

1 Give examples of **four** different types of additives and what they might be used for.

Check the facts

Manufacturers plan each product's processing to make profitable use of the team, factory plant and equipment.

The production process, from raw ingredients to storage of the finished product, must be smooth and efficient.

This chart shows how a manufacturer might plan the production process.

flow process chart	*possible use of control systems*
raw ingredients	
check quality	
store raw ingredients	*temperature control*
transfer ingredients to processing	*materials handling*
process raw ingredients	
transfer to cooking process	*materials handling*
cook	*temperature control*
transfer to high risk area	*materials handling*
chill	*temperature control*
transfer to assembly	*materials handling*
assemble	
quality control	*check weighting*
packaging, labelling and coding	
transfer to storage	*materials handling*
store	*temperature control*

key
- ○ *an operation*
- ⇨ *transport/movement*
- □ *quality control*
- ▽ *storage*

Test yourself

1 Name **four** processes indicated in a flow process chart.

Check the facts

Large-scale manufacture starts with the delivery of raw materials from approved sources, coordinated so they arrive just before they are needed.

Raw materials and supplies

Laboratory and quality checks are carried out against the specification (e.g. the percentages of moisture, protein, fat or salt, and the colour, texture and flavour levels for the materials) to approve or reject the order.

All batches of raw material are coded and a **stock control system** ensures that materials are used in rotation, with the oldest being used up first. They will be stored under controlled conditions, appropriate to the ingredients.

When a manufacturer has a new product idea, they will consider:

- What equipment do I currently have?
- What can the current equipment make?
- Can attachments be bought to make the machine do more functions?
- Does the factory have the capacity to make a new product?
- Do processes need to be altered to make the new recipe work?
- Are raw materials easily available or are they seasonal?
- Do the ingredients or final product need special storage or handling?

Test yourself

1 Why is the delivery of raw materials coordinated and controlled?

2 What is a 'stock control system'?

Check the facts

Production involves the careful management of resources, equipment and time.

Time is an important consideration for food manufacturers. The raw ingredients often arrive at the factory and are processed into the finished product within 24 hours! This is because fresh food ingredients have to be used quickly or they deteriorate, and because once the product is finished it has to be delivered to the consumer quickly to be eaten at its best.

Sequencing tasks

The food industry uses **Gantt charts** to sequence all the tasks, like the one shown below:

activities	*week 1*	*week 2*	*week 3*	*week 4*
market research				
evaluating				
generating ideas				
testing out ingredients				
modelling ideas				
advertising labelling				
packaging				
final recipe				
promotional video				

Test yourself

1 Why do manufacturers sequence tasks carefully?

2 What is a 'Gantt chart'?

Critical path analysis

Check the facts

Sometimes it is necessary to plan in more detail and to allow for a degree of flexibility. A critical path analysis chart may, therefore, be used.

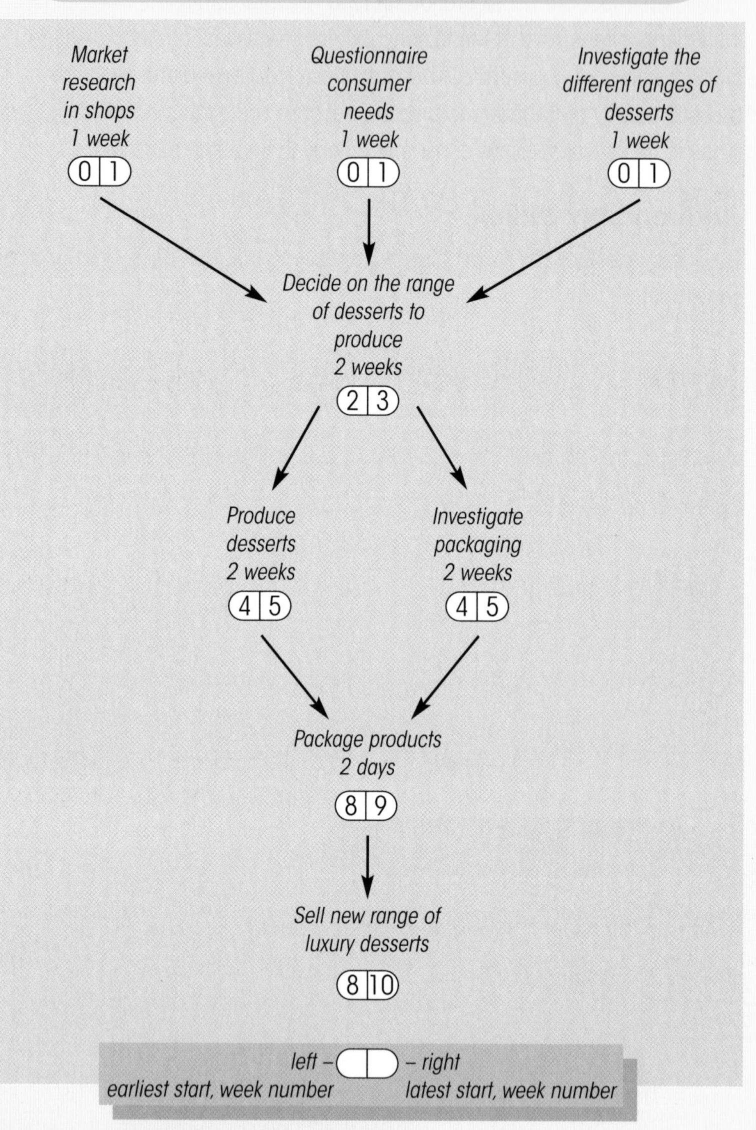

Test yourself

1 What is 'critical path analysis'?

Check the facts

The aim of food manufacturers is to produce products fit for human consumption and meet various needs. There are different scales of production, e.g. one-off production, batch production, mass production and continuous production.

Most food products are manufactured by one or more of the following methods – each of these **scales of production** requires different **machinery**, **tools** and **equipment**:

- **one-off**, **prototype** or **individual production**, for example a crafted product by a chef
- **batch production** – repetitive, small-scale manufacture of the same product by a team
- **mass production** – large-scale manufacturing on a production line where the process is split into a number of steps
- **continuous production** – large-scale manufacturing on a production line dedicated to one product, which may run uninterrupted 24 hours a day, seven days a week. However, production is stopped at regular intervals for cleaning, maintenance and quality inspections.

On the industrial scale, some manufacturing processes may be carried out in a similar way to food production at school or home, while some require more specialised industrial equipment.

Test yourself

1 What is meant by 'one-off production'?

2 What is the difference between 'batch' and 'mass production'?

Check the facts

Making consistent products, which don't vary in quality from an accepted standard, is very important in the food industry.

Throughout the manufacturing process, food products are subject to strict quality checks, to ensure that the products meet the agreed quality standards – getting it right first time, every time. This quality assurance should be distinguished from quality control, which involves inspection and testing at the end of the process.

HACCP (Hazard Analysis and Critical Control Point) is one particular quality assurance process that is used by the food industry. It takes a systematic approach to identifying hazards and risks, defining the means for their control. Developing HACCP assists companies to comply with legislation, supports due diligence and fulfils customer requirements for a food safety management system.

HACCP is:

- **systematic** – all the potential hazards are identified before there is a problem
- **efficient** – it concentrates the control effort at the stages where the risk is potentially highest
- **on-the-spot** – the process can be controlled immediately by the food business.

An operating manual for each product line will contain instructions for all stages in manufacture. This is a reference point for quality assurance and for training staff to the exact procedures and processes required. It will conform to the international standard **ISO 9000**.

Test yourself

1 What is the difference between 'quality control' and 'quality assurance'?

2 What does HACCP stand for?

Check the facts

HACCP analyses the entire manufacturing process and works out where hazards could occur and their risk level. It identifies those risks which are critical and sets up, and puts in place, controls to deal with this. It monitors the controls in use, to ensure that the system and controls are working.

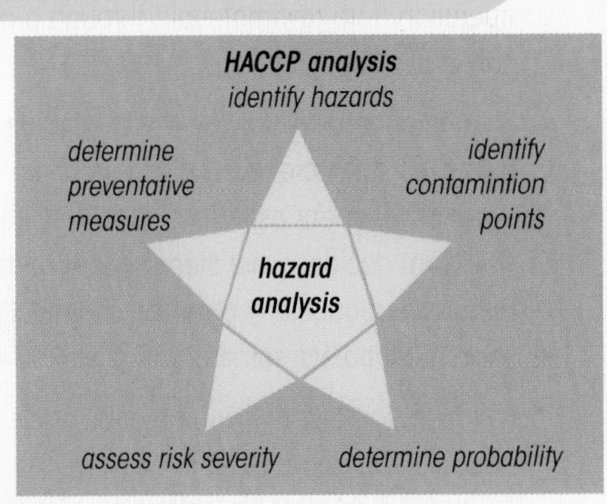

Identify and analyse hazards

Potential hazards associated with a food and measures to control those hazards are identified. The hazard could be biological such as a microbe; chemical, such as a toxin; or physical, such as metal fragments.

Identify critical control points

Critical control points (CCPs) are the points in a food's production – from its raw state through processing and shipping to consumption by the consumer – at which the potential hazard can be controlled or eliminated. Examples are cooking, cooling, packaging and metal detection.

Establish preventative measures

Preventative measures need to have critical limits for each control point. For a cooked food, for example, this might include setting a minimum cooking temperature and time required to ensure the elimination of many harmful microbes.

Establish procedures to monitor the critical control points

Such procedures might include determining how and by whom the cooking time and temperature should be monitored.

Establish corrective actions

Action must be taken when monitoring shows a critical control limit has not been met, for example, disposing of food if a metal has been detected.

Establish effective record keeping

Good records are essential to document the HACCP system.

Test yourself

1 What are the main stages of setting up HACCP?

2 What does CCP stand for?

93 How is HACCP set up?

Check the facts

When a HACCP team is formed, it should be made up of people who know and understand the business's food processes and product, food hygiene and microbiology.

1. The team draw up a flow chart showing all aspects of the food operation from raw materials, through processing, to storage and consumer handling.
2. The team identifies any potential hazards associated with the food at all stages, from the raw materials to the point at which the food is eaten. A risk assessment estimates how likely it is that a problem might occur. The team decides what steps should be taken to control the process to remove or reduce any physical, chemical or microbiological risks. These are control points, some of which will be **critical control points** (CCPs).
3. For each control point, in particular each CCP, the team recommends what is to be done, when it is to be done and who is to do it.
4. The recommended monitoring and controls must be carried out. Records of the HACCP process and the controls monitored at the CCP for each batch of food must be kept to show that the system is being implemented.
5. The design and running of the HACCP scheme should be reviewed whenever the food operation is altered and from time to time (e.g. once a year) to ensure maintenance of standards.

Test yourself

1. Who should make up a HACCP team?
2. What is a 'control point'?
3. Why should records be kept?

Check the facts

ICT is used to monitor and control processes more efficiently during production and manufacture of products.

Detection systems

Computerised control systems can rapidly detect and identify micro-organisms and metal (e.g. by X-ray inspection). Computer sensors and detectors all result in faster and more accurate quality control.

Sensors

Sensors are used to monitor conditions that must be regulated to ensure safe manufacture and to minimise waste, such as temperature, pH and weight. ICT provides feedback to control the system. For example, sensors are used to ensure that a cook-chill meal of pasta and sauce has the right amount of each element. If not, it is removed from the production line.

Robotics

Robots are used routinely for tasks that require repetitive actions and on production lines that run 24 hours a day. Robots are fast, very precise and have great strength; they are effective in increasing product output. They can be used for heavy, unpleasant and repetitive tasks, e.g. cutting blocks of frozen fish, and for fine manoeuvres, such as decorating a biscuit.

Digital imaging

Digital images are sent to the computer where it monitors the size, shape and position of ingredients on top of food products, e.g. pizza. When used in conjunction with robotics, changes in production can be made instantly.

Stock control

Factories and stores monitor stock control by computer and can forecast demand and sales, e.g. an increase in sales of drinks in warm weather.

Sensory analysis

Tasters can record their results directly into a computer. The data is processed and the results analysed quickly and easily.

Test yourself

1 Name **three** ways that computers are used in the manufacturing process.

2 Give **two** advantages of using computers to monitor and control production during manufacturing.

Process control

Check the facts

Process control monitors production in order to: make food products efficiently and safely; improve consistency; reduce human error and waste; avoid 'down time'; improve safety and hygiene and increase production efficiency.

A system is a sequence of events which has:
- inputs, e.g. ingredients
- processes, e.g. chopping, forming, cooking
- outputs, e.g. food products.

Process control works by:
- looking at a part of a process, e.g. chocolate flowing in a pipe
- monitoring that process, e.g. checking its temperature
- deciding when to make a change, e.g. if the temperature is too low
- making the change, e.g. raising the temperature.

Many parts of a process or product are controlled, including:
- weight of an individual item or mix of products
- temperature
- pH
- moisture content.

In order to manufacture products consistently, safely and efficiently, process control is used to monitor a number of sub-systems.

Test yourself

1 Give an example of a system, when making a food product, with an input, output and process.

2 How does process control work?

Check the facts

Computers monitor and control food production. This may involve automatic sensing and possible minor adjustments to the process conditions of a sub-system while production is still running. This is continuous monitoring.

Process control monitors a part of a production system, for example:

1. Sensing the critical parts of a process, e.g. the temperature of milk flowing through a pipe.

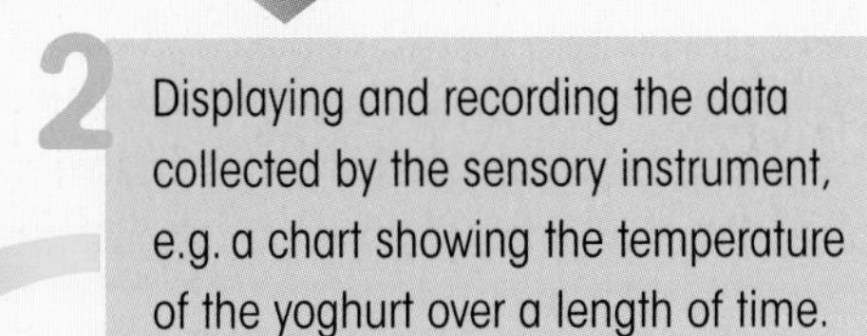

2. Displaying and recording the data collected by the sensory instrument, e.g. a chart showing the temperature of the yoghurt over a length of time.

3. Taking a decision – if the sensors detect that a specific part of the process is not within tolerance levels, a signal is sent to make a change, e.g. if the temperature drops too low, the product in the pipe may start to solidify and stop flowing (this is continuous monitoring).

4. Making a change to correct the faulty part, e.g. increase the temperature of the product in the pipe by a thermostat switching on a heater.

Test yourself

1 What is 'continuous monitoring'?

Continuous monitoring 2

Check the facts

During continuous monitoring, a series of things are monitored and controlled.

What is monitored and controlled?

The **weight** of an individual item, mix, package or mixture of products can be monitored and controlled.

The **flow rate** of ingredients. The method used to measure the flow of a fluid depends greatly on its composition. For example, some systems would not be suitable for fluids containing lumps, such as vegetable soup, as they would prevent the flow gauge from operating.

Temperature is a critical measurement for many food products, especially those that need to be sterilised or cooked, or cooled within a pre-determined time length, e.g. cook-chill meals.

The **composition**, for example, the solids content of a variety of liquid products, e.g. fruit juices, milk and syrups by measuring their refractive index. This is important when determining a product's composition or in the control of blending. This method may also be used to monitor product viscosity, e.g. the thickness of jam.

Test yourself

1 Name **three** things that are monitored and controlled.

Check the facts

Skillful packaging means that the product's quality can be assured once it has been manufactured. Care also needs to be taken of the product during distribution and storage.

Many food products are packaged using a combination of materials, e.g. foil, plastics and cardboard, which are assembled in a variety of ways.

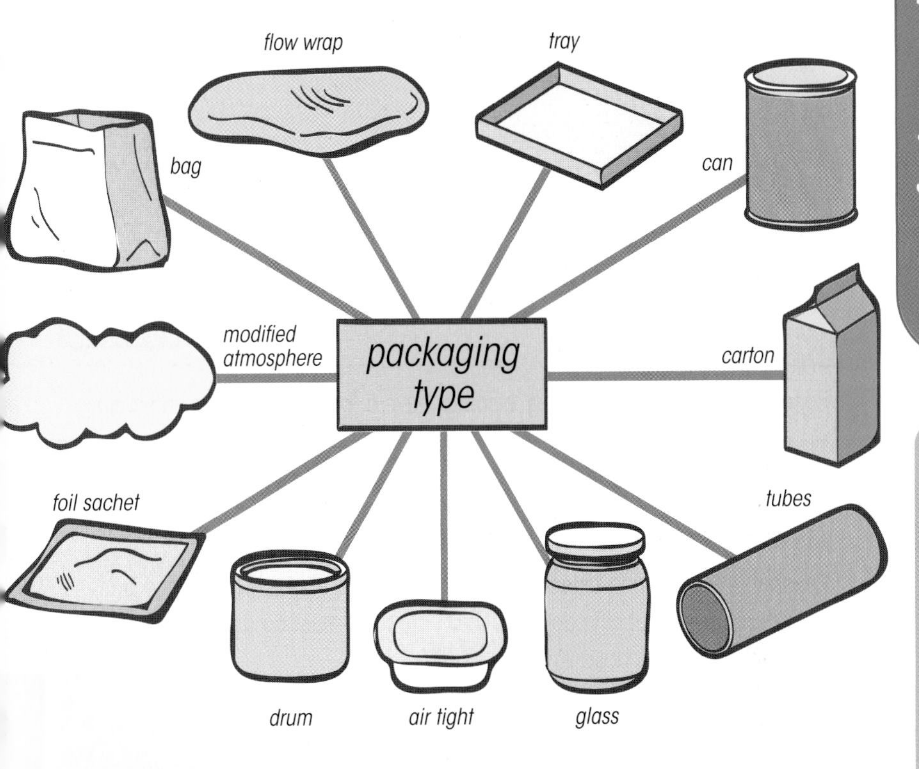

Test yourself

1 List **four** different types of food packaging.

Check the facts

Labels provide information about a product. When a manufacturer designs a label there is information that legally needs to be placed on the label.

The labels on all food products must contain:
- name or description of the food
- list of ingredients, in weight descending order
- date code
- special conditions of storage or use
- weight/volume in the pack
- place of origin if relevant
- name and address of the manufacturer, packer or EC seller
- special preparation or cooking instructions.

Best before

Foods with a long shelf-life, e.g. biscuits, have a 'best before' date, indicating by when the food should be eaten in order to be at its best. Food eaten after the date is unlikely to cause illness but may not be in peak condition.

Use by

Perishable foods, such as cold, cooked meats, are marked with a 'use by' date that gives a specific date by which the food must be used. Food used after the date may cause illness.

Nutritional labelling

This is not required by law unless a nutritional claim is made, but many manufacturers produce this information on the pack voluntarily.

Test yourself

1 What things must be on the food label by law?

2 What is the difference between 'use by' and 'best before' dates?

Check the facts

Modified atmosphere packaging (MAP) and aseptic packaging are ways to pack foods to extend their shelf-life.

Modified atmosphere packaging (MAP) is a method of packaging foods that extends the shelf-life by delaying microbial spoilage. It involves changing or modifying the usual atmosphere that would surround the food. The oxygen in the atmosphere, which is needed for microbial growth, is removed and replaced with carbon dioxide and nitrogen. Combined with low temperatures, it can reduce the need for less-popular methods of preservation, such as the addition of artificial preservatives. It can be used for a whole range of foods from prepared salads, vegetables and fruit to bread, fresh pasta and meat.

Aseptic packaging is a method of sterilising foods, then packaging them in sterile conditions. This destroys harmful bacteria which are present in the product and prevents any more from entering once the product has been sealed.

Test yourself

1 What is 'modified atmosphere packaging'?

2 What is 'aseptic packaging'?

01 Writing a design brief

1 (and 2)

New (original); **salad** (mixture of fresh fruit and/or vegetables); **looks good** (bright, mixed colours, effective packaging, attractive shapes); **appeals** (visual – makes you stop and look – good taste and smell, unusual); **customers** (consumers, those you buy for others, those who eat it); **sold in supermarkets** (chilled cabinet, delicatessen, or canned); **fruit and vegetables** (fresh fruit, roots, leaves, berries); **low fat** (not oily); **salad dressing** (thick liquid to pour over to mix, coat, add flavour); **accompany** (to go with salad, serve separately in sachet/bottle).

02 Writing an outline specification

1 A specification is a detailed statement describing a product.
2 An outline specification is an initial specification developed after early market research, highlighting possibilities and restrictions. It has open statements and changes as information is found out, ideas develop and are evaluated. It is a guide to the design process and prototype ideas. Final product specifications show finished product standards and are precise lists of requirements. They set the standard of ingredients, processes and finished products, ensuring all products are a consistent standard. It is a checklist and part of quality assurance and quality control procedures.
3 When a specification is developed the product is prototyped, modified and refined. The specification becomes more precise, until the final product specification is reached.

03 Where do new design ideas come from?

1 New/improved products are important for food manufacturers to make profits and be competitive. New products may replace old ones if sales have fallen off, and can help increase sales volumes. It is important for manufacturers to develop and keep a good profile, or portfolio of recognisable products, to build a brand image.
2 A 'new food' product is one that has never been designed and made before – a new flavour, a modification to a standard product, e.g. improvement, new pack size or cost reduction, or an addition to an existing range of products. It has been argued that no design is totally original and most are based on products which already exist.
3 About 7000 new food products are launched each year.

04 Concept development

1 A concept is a general idea about a food product to inspire new products.
2 Concept development is a creative process, forming vague, early ideas into clearer ones to further develop a product.
3 You can use questioning, product analysis, recipe books, mood boards, brainstorming and attribute analysis.

05 Concept screening

1 Concept screening filters ideas and tests the feasibility of a new product.
2 The process starts with marketing and product development teams brainstorming. The ideas are filtered (screened) through various stages becoming fewer and more focused. Ideas are tested to see if they are realistic. The best ideas are narrowed down to one that seems most worthwhile to develop and this is put forward for development.
3 The innovation funnel model used by Birds' Eye Walls is an example of a process to test and evaluate a number of ideas. It has stages or decision points to eliminate those ideas that are not good enough.
4 90% failure rate.

06 Consumer preference

1 'Aesthetics' describes a sensory response to food (sight, hearing, taste and smell).
2 Subjective tests collect information about people's likes and dislikes.
3 A consumer panel involves gathering a group of people likely to purchase or consume the product and finding out their opinions and feelings about the product and its packaging.

07 Analysing existing food products

1 Market intelligence is an awareness of competitors' products and what is new on the supermarket shelf.
2 Attribute analysis involves analysing an existing product to get ideas for a new product, to examine how it has been made, or to understand its features (attributes) further. For example, what ingredients and processes are used, what are its successful features and how could it be improved?

08 Testing and evaulating products

1 Evaluation is testing ideas and new products throughout the designing process to refine the end product. As a product is modelled, tested and trialled, it is constantly adapted and improved.
2 Nutritional analysis involves working out a nutritional profile for a product.
3 Preference tests are subjective and indicate how much a product is liked or disliked.
4 Objective tests are discrimination tests where samples are compared to find out whether any differences are detectable between them, e.g. sweetness of a product.

09 What is sensory evaluation?

1 Sensory evaluation involves tasters looking at, smelling and eating food samples; then recording their opinions.
2 Sight, smell, taste, mouthfeel/touch, hearing.
3 A fair test should be set up. Tasters shouldn't be distracted or influenced, so use individual booths, free from cooking smells and with controlled lighting; prepare same-sized samples in identical dishes at the correct temperature, coded with random numbers. Provide water and crackers to eat between samples.

10 How is sensory evaluation used?

1 Sensory evaluation checks the quality of existing products and develops new ones.
2 During development of prototypes, sensory evaluation checks the specification is being met and the impact of improvements.
3 Sensory evaluation tests samples at known periods of time after production to see if the eating quality is affected.
4 Sensory evaluation is used to check if there are differences across batches of products made to maintain consistency and to ensure they meet the original specification.

11 Preference tests

1 Paired comparison is a preference test, asking which of two samples tasters prefer.
2 A ranking test is a preference test, asking tasters to rank the samples in order of preference – most liked to least liked.
3 Hedonic ranking is a preference test, which asks tasters to score their preference for each sample on a 5- or 9-point scale.

12 Discrimination tests

1 Discrimination tests are objective tests that aim to evaluate specific attributes.
2 Triangle tests use three samples (two are identical). Tasters try to find the odd one out.

13 Star diagrams and profiling

1 Profile
2 Colour, flavour, overall acceptability, volume, smell.

14 Designing with ICT 1

1 Computers are used to handle information, model ideas, calculate information and communicate ideas to other people.
2 The ingredients and their nutritional content are displayed in a spreadsheet. You can change the ingredients and the spreadsheet will recalculate the new nutritional content.

15 Designing with ICT 2

1 Computer software is used to model bacterial growth in food products and work out safe production and shelf life.
2 Software packages can be used to design nets and graphics used on packaging, e.g. photos, logos, name, ingredients, weight and nutritional information.
3 Virtual reality can show how products might look on supermarket shelves or how a design for a new cake decoration might look.

16 Recipe engineering

1a The recipe could be altered to use:
- roast turkey (breast and dark meat)
- sliced cooked chipolatas
- sliced steamed carrots
- gravy
- piped mashed potato.

1b This combination is less labour intensive with shorter cooking times and therefore cheaper to manufacture in large amounts

17 From outline specification to final product specifiation

1 Initial brief, market research, design brief, initial specification, generation of ideas, concept screening, product prototyping and development, sensory evaluation and viability testing, modification, final product specification.
2 Description of product; detailed ingredients weight/size; recipe; nutritional information; HACCP flow chart; quality standards; visual appearance; taste panel results; product life.

3 The range of acceptable amounts, e.g. 50 % white flour (±2 %), means that anywhere between 48–52 % would be acceptable.

18 Choosing the right materials

1 Each material in a food product is selected for a particular function. The choice of materials for a food product is influenced by the type of product, the price that will be charged and the processing.
2 **Flour**: bulking, provides energy and fibre, gluten in coagulation (sets the biscuit) and dextrinisation of starch; **Butter**: is a carrier for fat soluble viatmins A and D (these are added by law to margarine as not carried naturally) moistens, adds colour and flavour, provides energy and fat-soluble vitamins, shortening; **Oats**: crumbliness, provides energy and fibre, bulking; **Sugar**: sweetens, adds colour and flavour, caramelisation, aeration; **Eggs**: texture, provides protein and fat, aeration and coagulation.

19 Protein

1 Protein is made up of amino acids.
2 Amino acids are compounds that contain carbon, hydrogen, oxygen and nitrogen.
3 They perform different functions because the amino acids are joined in a particular order.
4 Collagen: meat, gluten: flour, albumen: egg.

20 Functional properties of protein

1 Denaturation is the unfolding of protein molecules due to heat, salts, pH and mechanical action, e.g. whisking.
2 When heated, proteins unfold from their coiled state and form a solid stable network.
3 Coagulation can be used for thickening sauces, binding ingredients together, making cheese and yoghurt.

21 Gluten formation

1 Two proteins in wheat flour, gliadin and glutenin, mix with water to form gluten.
2 'Developing the gluten' means untangling the gluten strands and aligning them, for example by kneading.
3 Gluten is strong and elastic. It gives structure by trapping gases that expand on cooking.

22 Carbohydrates

1 Monosaccharides are the simplest carbohydrate molecules,e.g. glucose, fructose and galactose.
2 Disaccharides are formed from two monosaccharide molecules, by eliminating a molecule of water, e.g. sucrose (glucose + fructose), lactose (glucose + galactose), and maltose (glucose + glucose).
3 Polysaccharides are made up of many monosaccharide molecules, joined together, e.g. starch, glycogen, cellulose and pectin.

23 Functional properties of carbohydrates

1 When foods containing starch are baked or roasted, dextrinisation (a browning process) occurs, forming dextrin. This is the Maillard reaction (protein and a reducing sugar). The colour, flavour and smell changes, e.g. toast, bread and croissants.
2 Caramelisation occurs when sugar is heated above its melting point, forming caramel.
3 Gelatinsation is a thickening process. When starch is mixed with water and heated, the starch granules swell, absorbing the liquid.

24 Fats

1 Fats are made of glycerol and fatty acids.
2 Monounsaturated fatty acids have one carbon double bond, polyunsaturated fatty acids have more than one double bond.
3 Hydrogenation is a process of hardening fats and oils, as in margarine manufacture and production of low-fat spreads.

25 Functional properties of fat

1 Fat coats the flour particles so they can't abosorb water, reducing gluten development.
2 Plasticity describes the melting point of a particular fat. Products have low melting points so are easy to spread from the fridge.
3 Fat can be creamed with sugar to incorporate small air bubbles and form a foam.

26 Colloidal systems

1 Colloidal systems give structure, texture and mouthfeel to products.
2 Colloids form when one substance disperses though another without mixing or combining.
3 The main types of colloidal systems are sols, gels, emulsions and foams.

27 Sols and gels

1 Sols are a mixture of solid particles dispersed in liquid; sometimes heated and stirred.
2 A gel is formed when a sol is heated and cooled and forms a solid.
3 Syneresis is the weeping of a gel.

28 Emulsions
1 Emulsions are formed when two liquids that don't usually mix are held together in a stable state.
2 Immiscible means it won't mix and separates on standing, e.g. oil and water.
3 Emulsifying agents hold an emulsion in a stable state, e.g. egg yolk in mayonnaise.

29 Foams
1 A foam is made of small air bubbles, dispersed in a liquid, e.g. whisked cream.
2 When a foam is heated, protein sets the structure to form a solid, e.g. meringue.

31 The basics of raising agents
1 Raising agents produce gas that expands on cooking, e.g. whisking/baking powder.
2 Three gases that makes food rise are air, steam and CO_2.

32 Air as a raising agent
1 Sieving, folding and rolling, creaming, whisking, rubbing-in and beating.
2 **Flaky pastry** – sieving, rubbing-in, folding, rolling; **scones** – sieving, rubbing-in; **cakes** – sieving, creaming; **meringue** – whisking.

33 Steam as a raising agent
1 Steam expands 1600 times its original volume.
2 Mixtures should contain a lot of liquid and be cooked at a high temperature.

34 Carbon dioxide as a raising agent
1 Carbon dioxide is incorporated into mixtures using chemical (baking powder), or biological, raising agents, (yeast).
2 Baking powder is a commercial mix of bicarbonate of soda and an acid.
3 Yeast is added to bread dough and left to rise (prove). The yeast cells multiply by budding, which requires energy obtained from fermenting carbohydrate in the dough. The CO_2 gas formed causes the dough to rise.
4 On baking, dough rises by expanding CO_2 gas. The temperature rises, so yeast activity stops. The dough sets as gluten coagulates and starch gelatinises.

35 The basics of cake making
1 Methods of cake making are rubbing-in, creaming, melting and whisked.
2 The cakes are different because the ratio, type of ingredients and methods used vary.
3 The main ingredients for cake making are fat, sugar (or syrup or treacle), eggs, flour, raising agent, liquid and flavourings.

36 Rubbing-in method
1 The rubbing-in method is a process of rubbing in the fat to the flour with the fingertips until it resembles breadcrumbs.
2 Rubbing-in is used for fruit and rock cakes and scones.
3 The cakes are dry, open with short shelf life.
4 It uses half the amount of fat to flour.

37 Creaming method
1 Fat and sugar are creamed together before eggs are beaten in and flour added.
2 It is used for victoria sandwich, Madeira cake and sponge buns.
3 Light cakes.
4 Equal amounts of sugar, fat and flour to the weight of the eggs.

38 Melting method
1 The fat is melted with treacle, sugar and syrup before other ingredients are added.
2 Gingerbread, flapjacks, brownies.
3 Soft, sticky, moist cakes, long shelf life.
4 Up to half fat to flour, high proportion of sugar.

39 Whisked method
1 Eggs and sugar are whisked together, flour is gently folded in.
2 Swiss roll, sponge drops, sponge flan, sponge sandwich.
3 Very light soft cakes, short shelf life.
4 Half the amounts of sugar and flour to the weight of the eggs.

40 The basics of pastry making: shortcrust pastry
1 Shortcrust, flaky and choux.
2 Flour, fat, water.
3 Pasties, pies and tarts.

41 Flaky pastry
1 Flaky pastry is used for turnovers, cream horns, eccles cakes and sausage rolls.
2 Flaky pastry is crisp and layered, with a higher ratio of fat to flour than shortcrust pastry, which is light and short crumb. Flaky pastry is rolled and folded into layers; shortcrust is rubbed-in, mixed and rolled once.

42 Choux pastry
1 Eclairs, profiteroles, cheese puffs.
2 Fat and water are melted and heated to a rolling boil. Flour is added and heated to form a roux. Once cooled slightly, the eggs are beaten gradually into the mixture.

43 The basics of bread making

1 Flour, yeast, salt and liquid.
2 It is the raising agent.
3 Salt strengthens the gluten, controls the yeast and adds flavour.

44 Traditional bread making

1 The yeast produces CO_2 gas that causes the dough to rise.
2 The dough is thoroughly kneaded to release some of the gas and distribute the remaining gas bubbles, for a more evenly textured bread without large air holes.
3 Leave to rise for a second time before baking.

45 Commercial bread making

1 A large quantity of dough is made and left to ferment for three hours.
2 The first fermentation stage is replaced by intense mixing of the dough, which rapidly stretches the gluten.
3 It reduces factory space and time needed for bulk fermentation, produces higher yields and reduces costs, decreases staling rate and produces better quality bread.

46 Traditional and blended sauces

1 Sauces can be thickened by starch (white sauce/custard), by making a puree of fruit (raspberry sauce) or vegetables (tomato/onion) or by using eggs (egg custard).
2 Cornflour, arrowroot and liquid.
3 Mixing starch with a little liquid first.

47 Roux and all-in-one sauces

1 Flour, fat and liquid.
2 To prevent lumps in the sauce.

48 Nutrition

1 Nutrition is the study of nutrients and their relationship with food and living things.
2 Nutrients are chemical components needed by humans to maintain life and health.
3 The main nutrients are carbohydrate, fat, protein, vitamins and minerals.
4 Water is essential for all our body processes. Dietary fibre is not digested but aids digestion, adding bulk to the diet, assisting in removing waste products as faeces.

50 Healthy eating

1 A diagram of a dinner plate showing the proportions of the different food groups that people are advised to eat for a healthy diet.
2 Making sure you eat the right combinations of a variety of foods which provide the nutrients necessary for well-being.

52 Healthy eating guidelines

1 Enjoy food; eat a variety of foods; eat right amount to be a healthy weight for height; eat plenty of foods rich in starch and fibre; don't eat too much fat; don't eat sugary foods too often; store and prepare foods carefully to maintain vitamin and mineral content; keep alcohol within sensible limits.
2 A balanced diet, together with regular exercise, can help maintain a healthy body weight and may reduce the chances of developing diet-related illnesses, e.g. CHD.

53 Saving Lives: Our Healthier Nation

1 An action plan to tackle poor health.
2 Cancer, CHD and stroke, accidents and mental health.
3 Risk factors: poor diet, smoking, no exercise.

54 Nutrient intakes

1 DRVs are 'dietary reference values'. The figures indicate the amount of nutrients needed for different people in good health.
2 RNI means 'reference nutrient intake' – the amount of nutrient thought to cover the needs of most people in a particular group. It is the DRV for protein, vitamins and minerals.
3 EARs stands for 'estimated average requirements'. It is the DRV used for energy.

55 Nutrition throughout life

1 Nutritional needs vary, e.g. men and women have different needs; childhood involves rapid growth and development; more energy is required by physically-active people.
2 Vegetarian: no meat, fish, animal products. Weight loss: low calorie/fat/sugar intake. Lactose intolerant: no milk/diary products. Gluten intolerant (coeliac): no wheat.

56 Nutritional analysis with ICT

1 To calculate the nutritional content/profile; manipulate ratios; produce a graph/chart.

57 Meat

1 Muscle tissue of animals.
2 To soften collagen.
3 Reduce the length of the muscle fibre by mincing/hitting with a meat hammer or adding a tenderiser, such as a marinade.

58 Meat analogues

1 See page 63.
2 TVP, tofu, tempeh.
3 Myco-protein is fermented *Fusarium graminearum*.

59 Fish

1 Fish has less connective tissue.
2 It can be grouped by origin (fresh water; sea water), or fat content and type (white fish, oily fish, shellfish).

60 Eggs

1 Battery, deep litter, barn, free range.
2 Shell, white and yolk.
3 The yolk structure weakens, egg white gets thinner, air space increases, bacteria may enter through the shell, a bad egg smell.

61 Milk and milk products

1 Cream, yoghurt, cheese, butter.
2 An enzyme, called rennin, is used to clot milk and produce milk solids (casein curd) and liquid (whey), which is drained off. The different cheeses result from different production methods, e.g. pressing of the curd and ripening for hard cheese.
4 Brie, Gouda, Stilton, Cheddar, cottage, Ricotta.

62 Cereals

1 Grasses.
2 Foods that are cheap to produce and make up the bulk of the local diet.
3 Wheat, maize or corn, rice, oats, barley, rye.

63 Flour

1 Wholemeal flour uses the whole grain; white flour is refined – the bran is removed.
2 Soft flour contains 8 % protein and is suitable for cakes. Strong flour contains a maximum of 17 % protein and is used for yeast doughs, flaky, puff and choux pastry.
3 Fat and sugar.
4 Salt and ascorbic acid.

64 Fats and oils

1 At room temperature, fat: solid; oil: liquid.
2 Butter: spreading, biscuits, cakes, pastry, sauces; lard: pastry, roasting, frying; suet: puddings, dumplings, jam roly poly.
3 Oils: sunflower, soya, olive, corn – frying; margarine: sunflower, soya, olive – spreading, pastry.

65 Sugar

1 Sugar cane or sugar beet.
2 See chart on page 70.

66 Fruit and vegetables

1 See chart on page 71.
2 The cell has an outer wall of cellulose. In the cell, there is a jelly-like substance called cytoplasm that carries fat droplets and colour pigments. The major part of the cell (vacuole) contains cell sap, which is watery and contains sugar, pigments and salts. Between the cells there are small pockets (intercellular spaces) that give raw fruit and vegetables their opaqueness. On cooking, the cell structure breaks down and raw fruit and vegetables become softer.
3 Discolouration is enzymic browning, which can be slowed by antioxidants or blanching (to denature enxymes). Adding acidic/sugary solutions to the fruit's surface or keeping it at cold temperatures prevents it.

67 Heat exchange

1 Heat is applied to food to improve taste, smell and texture; prevent spoilage; increase keeping qualities; make food easier to digest.
2 Heat is removed from food to alter the appearance and texture, prevent spoilage and increase keeping qualities.
3 Heat can be exchanged by conduction (stir fry, ice cream), convection (boiling, blast chilling) and radiation (grilling, microwaving, sun drying).

68 Conduction, convection and radiation

1 Conduction is the exchange of heat by direct contact with food on a surface, e.g. stir-frying vegetables in a wok, pasteurising milk in a plate heat-exchanger.
2 Convection is heat exchange by applying a gas or liquid current, e.g. frying potatoes or freezing peas with a cold air blast.
3 Radiation is energy in the form of rays that pass through the air until they come into contact with food. Grilling involves the use of infra-red heat rays created by gas flames, charcoal or glowing electric elements.

69 Food hygiene

1 Pathogens are harmful bacteria that cause illness.
2 Pathogens come from a person's skin, mouth, ears, hair and gut; animals; raw foods; food waste and rubbish.
3 Pathogens need food, moisture, warmth and time to multiply.

70 Food poisoning

1 Food poisoning symptoms are feeling/being sick, diarrhoea and stomach pains.
2 Preparing food too far in advance; storing it at room temperature; thawing, cooling or

reheating inadequately; undercooking; eating raw food; keeping food warm (below 63 °C); infected food handlers, contaminated processed food, poor hygiene.

71 Food poisoning bacteria

1 See page 75.
2 *Listeria monocytogenes.*
3 *Staphylococcus aureus.*

72 How can you prevent food poisoning?

1 Wash hands; keep pets out of kitchen; keep foods covered; keep raw and cooked foods separate.
2 Control food storage temperature (below 5 °C; above 63 °C), to stop bacteria multiplying.
3 Cook thoroughly and through to the centre.

73 Food spoilage and safe storage

1 Raw meat should be stored separately from cooked foods and kept at the bottom of the fridge so no blood can drip and transfer pathogens onto ready-to-eat items.
2 5–63 °C
3 The operating temperatures of the fridge will rise if hot food is placed in it to cool, putting other foods in the fridge at risk.

74 Safe food handling

1 Wearing protective clothing; hair tied back and covered with a hairnet; removing rings, jewellery, watches and nail varnish.
2 Frozen foods must be totally defrosted before cooking to allow heat to completely penetrate.
3 Most pathogens are killed by cooking to a centre temperature of 72 °C for at least two minutes. This can be checked by using a thermometer, to ensure food is piping hot.

75 Principles of food preservation

1 Food preservation stops spoilage by micro-organisms or enzymic breakdown.
2 See page 80.

76 Methods of food preservation

1 Food was preserved for winter.
2 Traditionally, food was hung over wood fires to smoke it.
3 Nicholas Appert.

77 Pasteurisation

1 A form of heat processing.
2 Batch and high temperature pasteurisation.

78 Sterilisation

1 A severe form of heat processing that destroys most micro-organisms.
2 Some micro-organisms can form spores able to survive high temperatures. Temperatures over 100 °C will destroy them.

79 UHT

1 Ultra-heat treatment.
2 UHT kills mico-organisms without causing as much damage to the product as sterilisation.

80 Canning

1 Peas, beans, fruit, soups, meat.
2 Washing and preparing the food, blanching fruit/vegetables (boiling water), filling the cans, sealing the cans, heating in a retort, cooling and labelling with 'best before' date.
3 A retort is similar to a large pressure cooker.

81 Dehydration

1 Dehydration stops micro-organisms growing by making the water unavailable.
2 Fruit, vegetables, coffee, milk.
3 See page 86.

82 Freezing

1 Very low temperatures inhibit growth of micro-organisms, slowing down enzyme activity. Once frozen, water is unavailable to micro-organisms and prevent their growth.
2 See page 87.
3 See page 87.

83 Chilling

1 Reducing the temperature slows down the rate of decay.
2 Lasagne, cottage pie, chicken tikka masala, pies, pasta and sauce, potato salad.
3 Cook-chill products are prepared, cooked and chilled rapidly. They are usually made in batches. They are stored at a temperature just above 0 °C until they are sold.

84 Additives

1 They are additives that have passed strict safety tests and are only added to foods once known to be safe.

85 Types of additives

1 Preservatives, antioxidants and stabilisers prevent micro-organisms growing and extend shelf-life; colours can restore or enhance the colour of manufactured food; intense sweeteners can be added, e.g. diet lemonade; flavour enhancers can bring out the flavour, e.g. monosodium glutamate (E621).